Bird's Journey

Coloring Book
for all ages

OANCEA CAMELIA

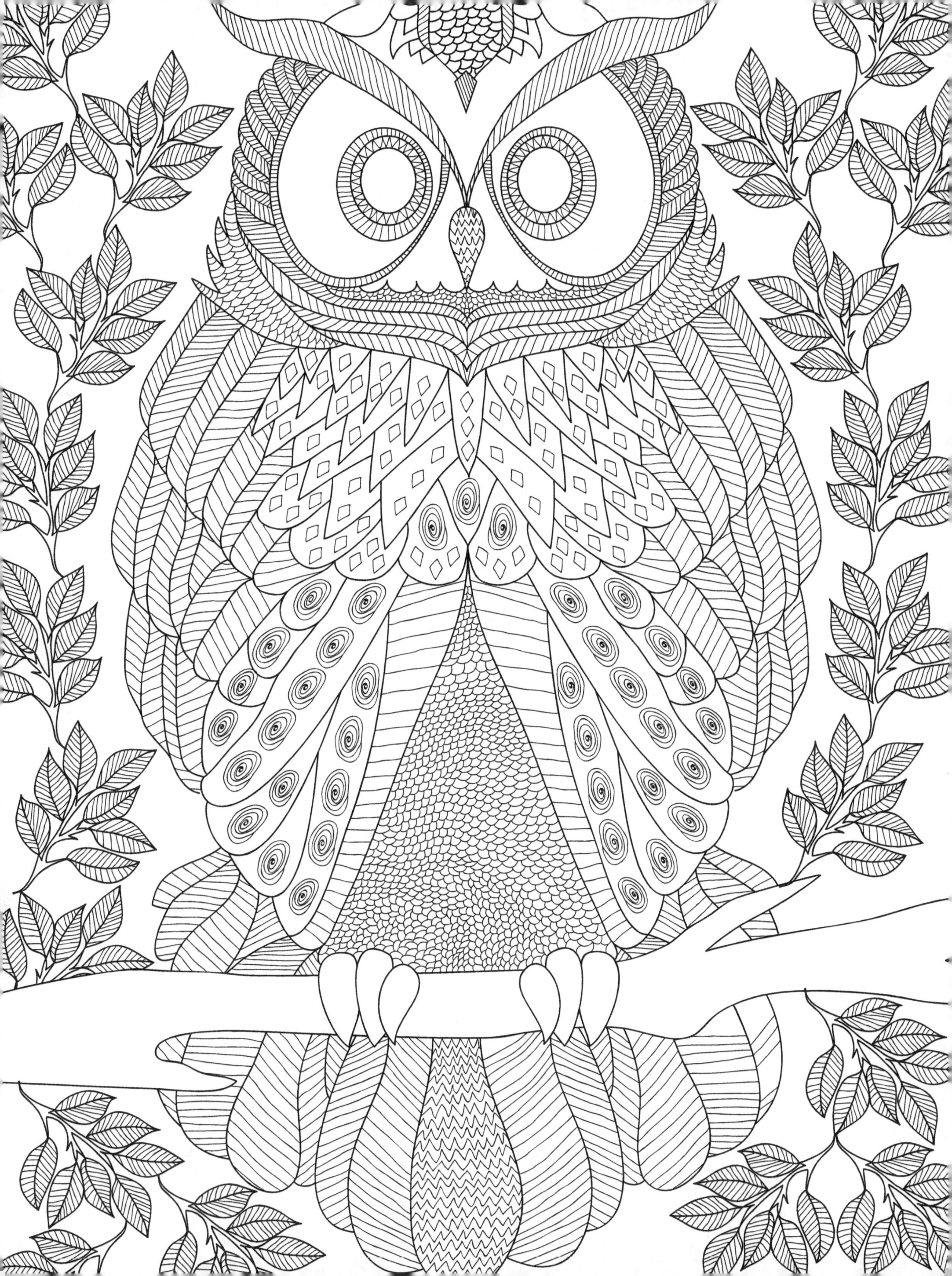

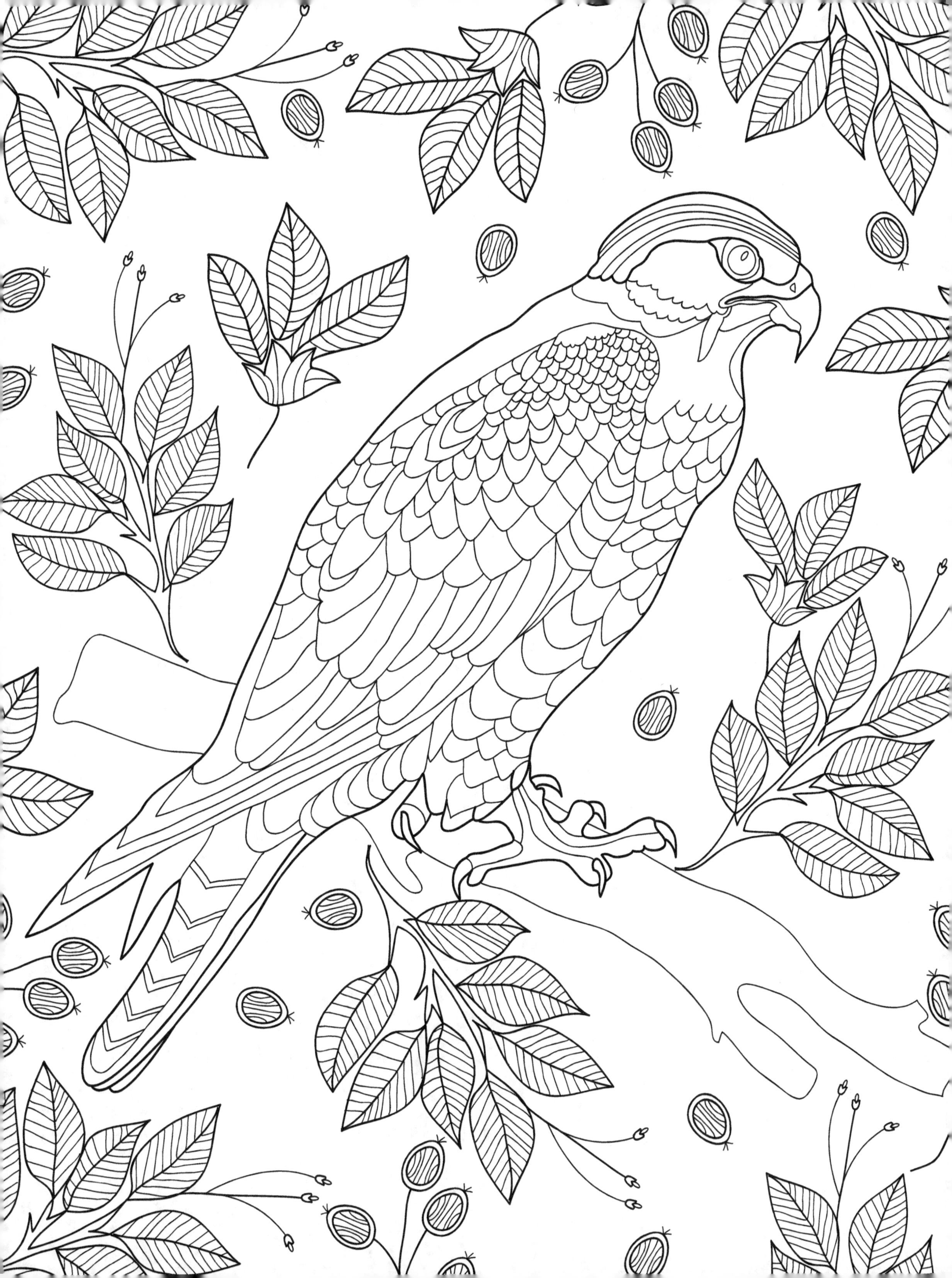

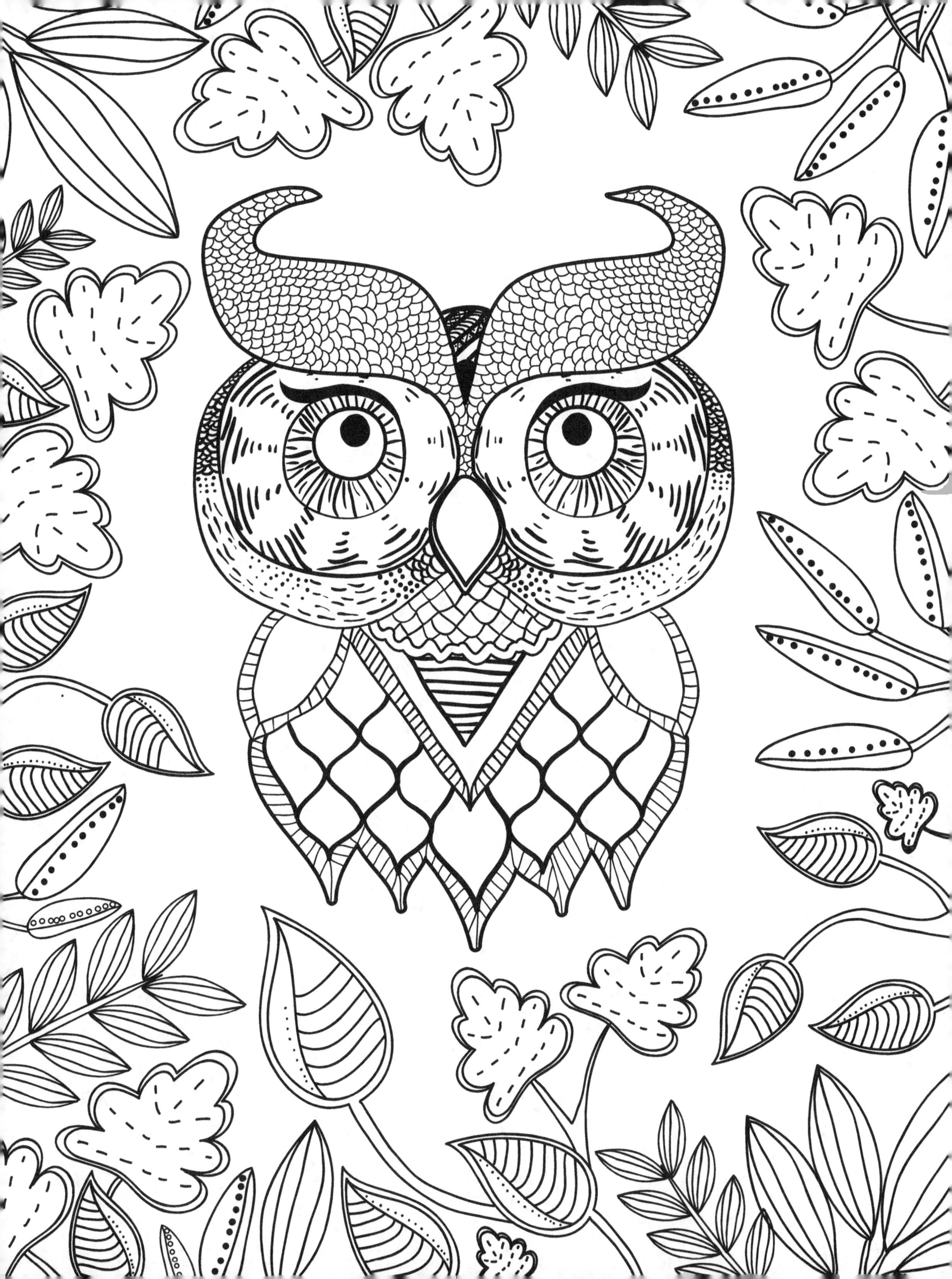

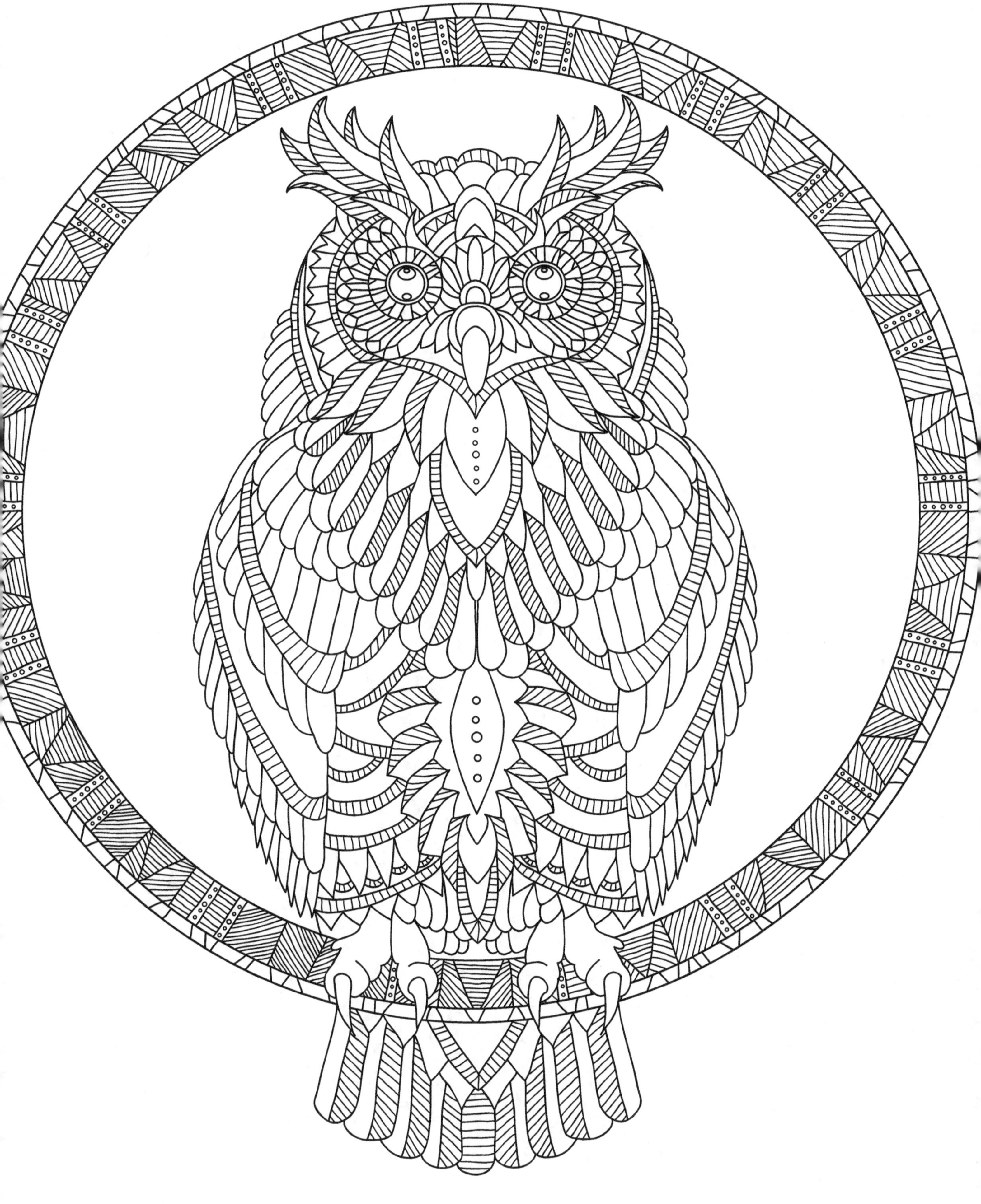

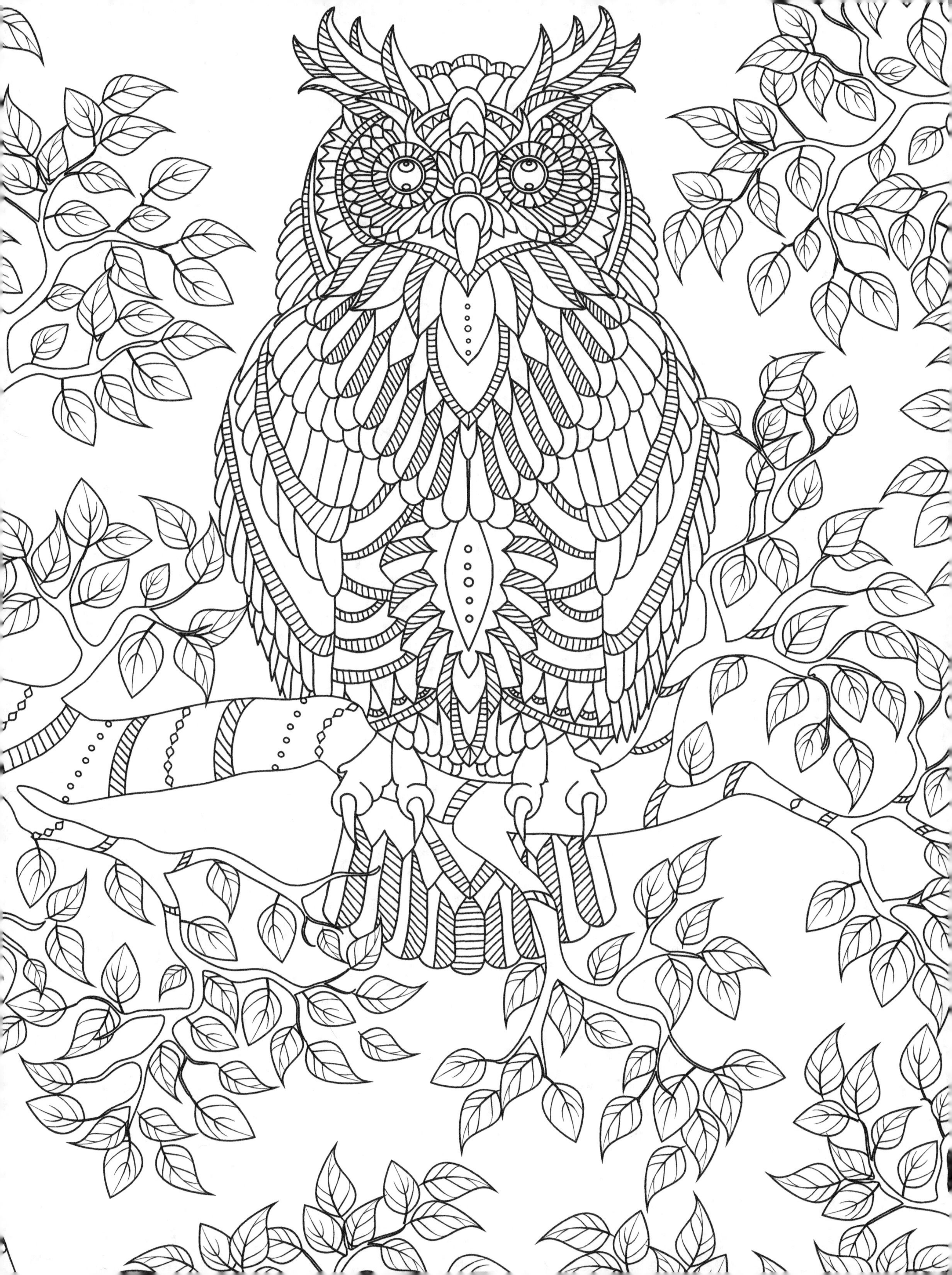

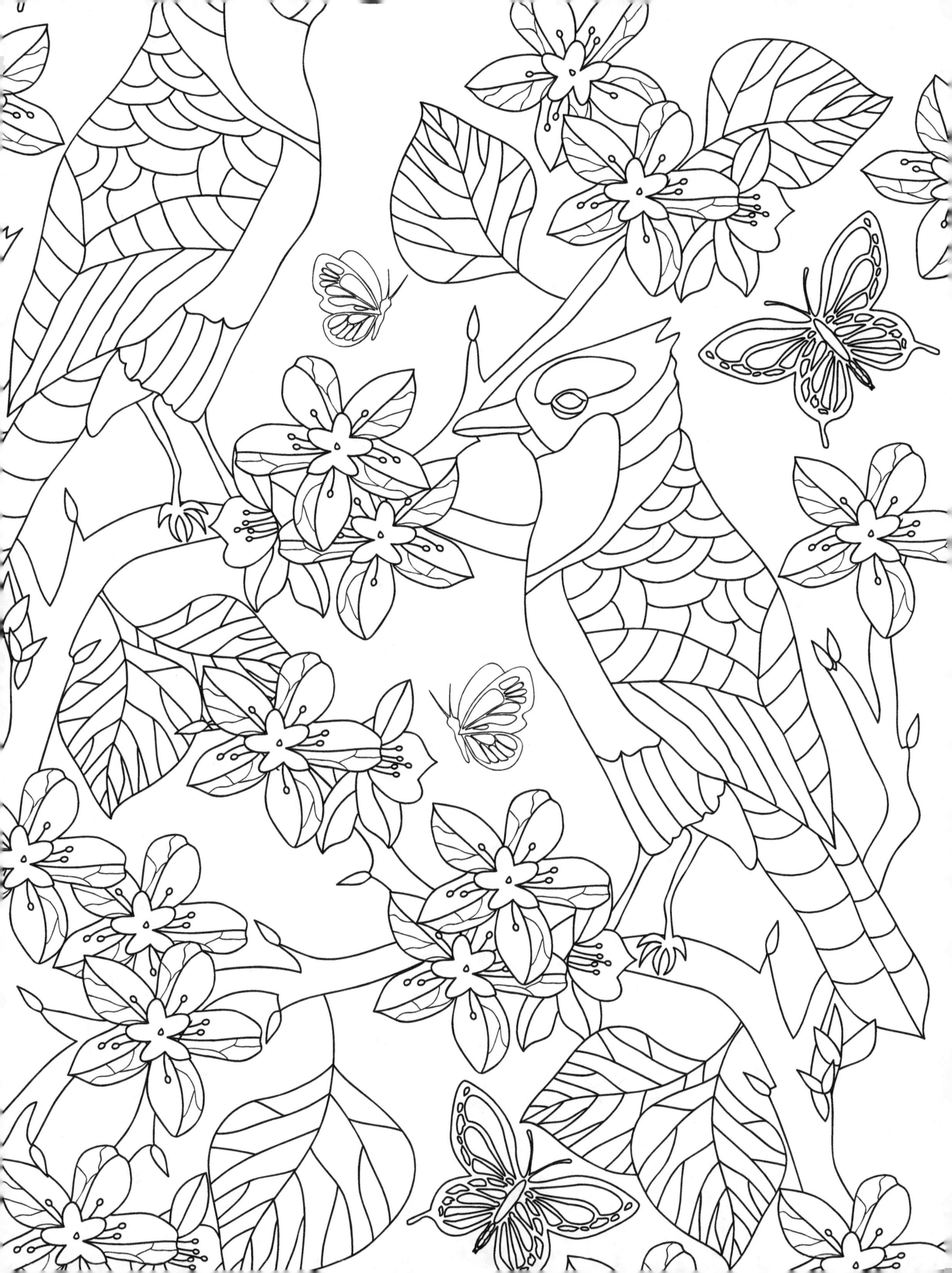

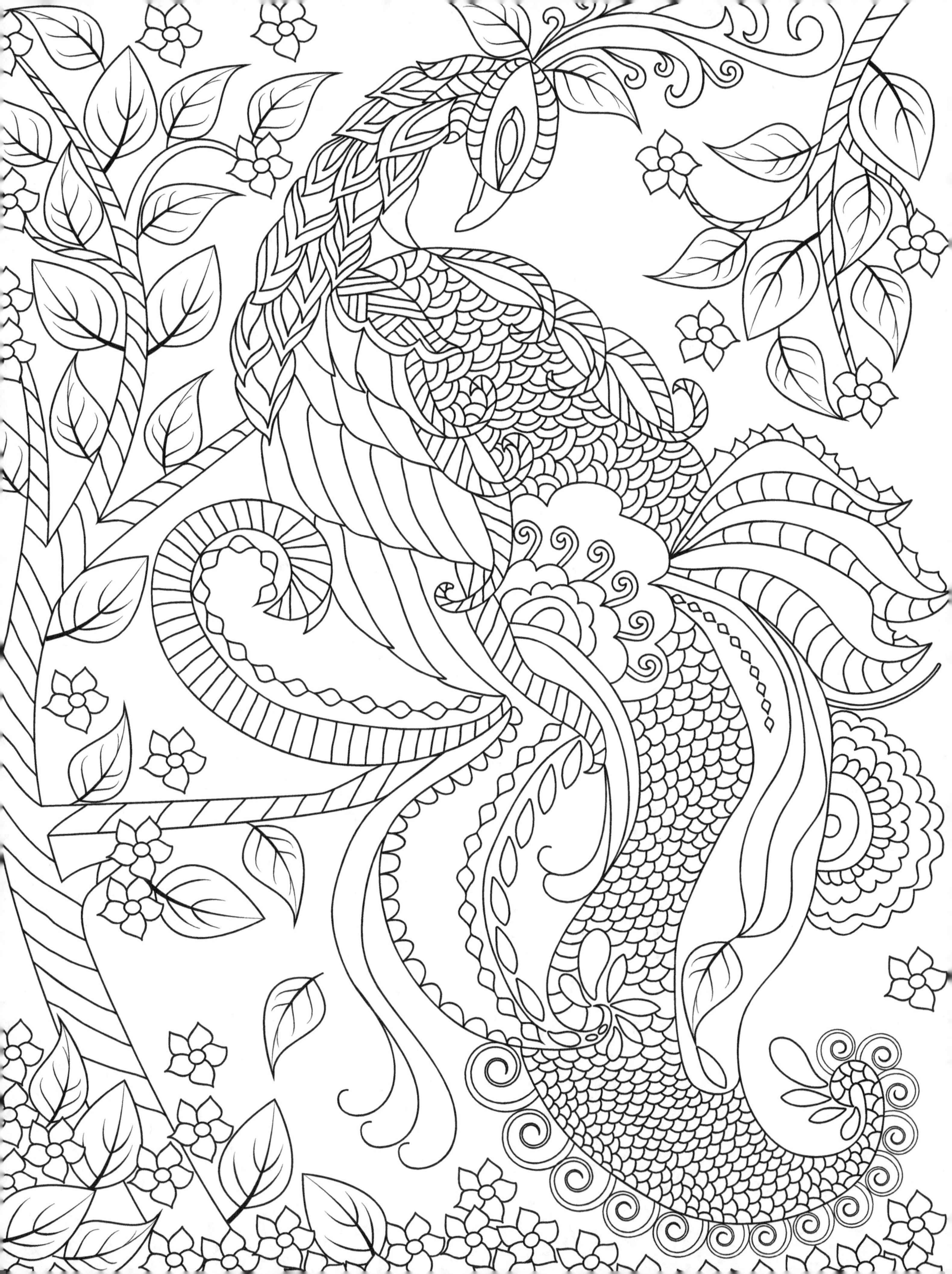

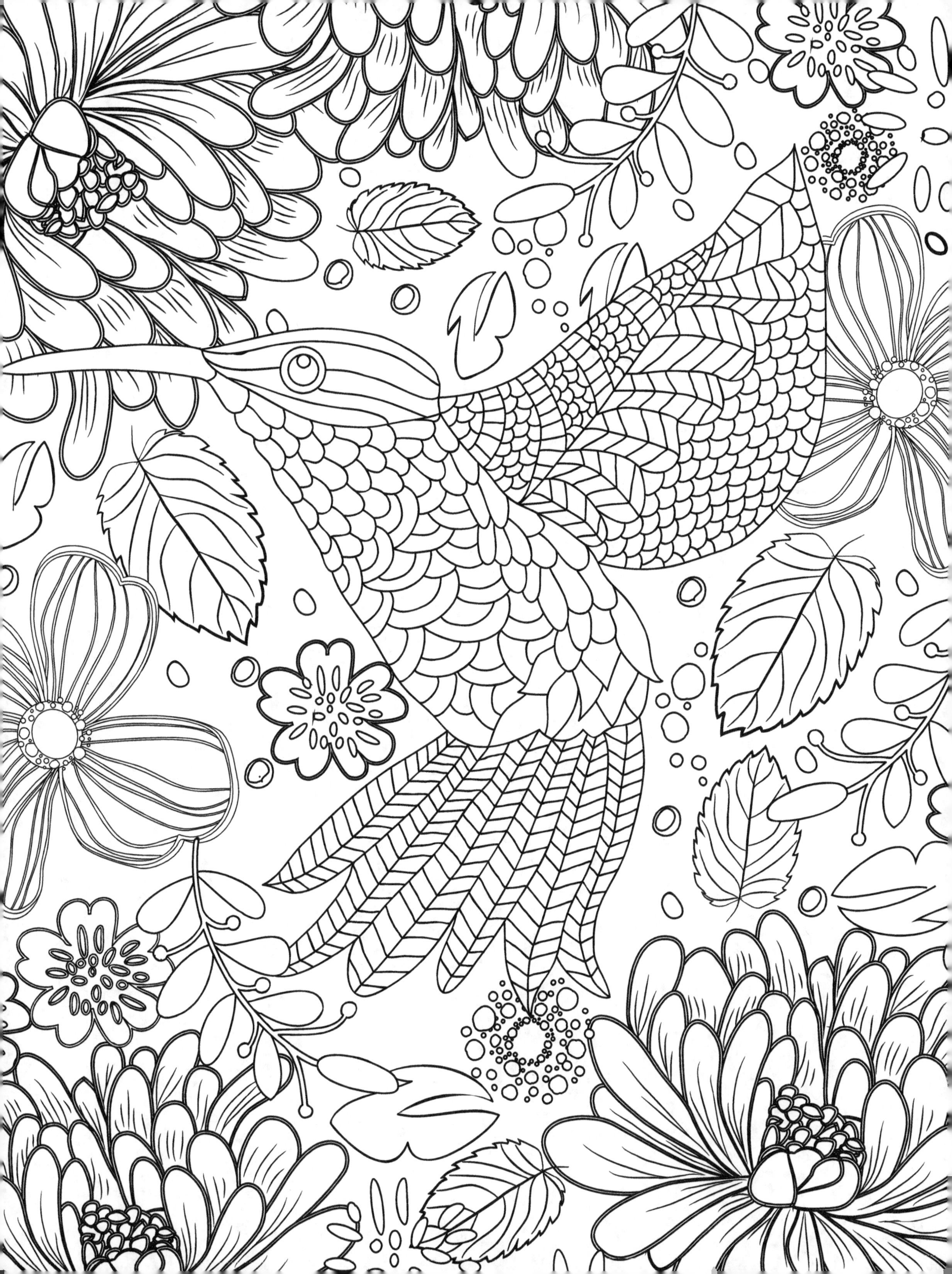

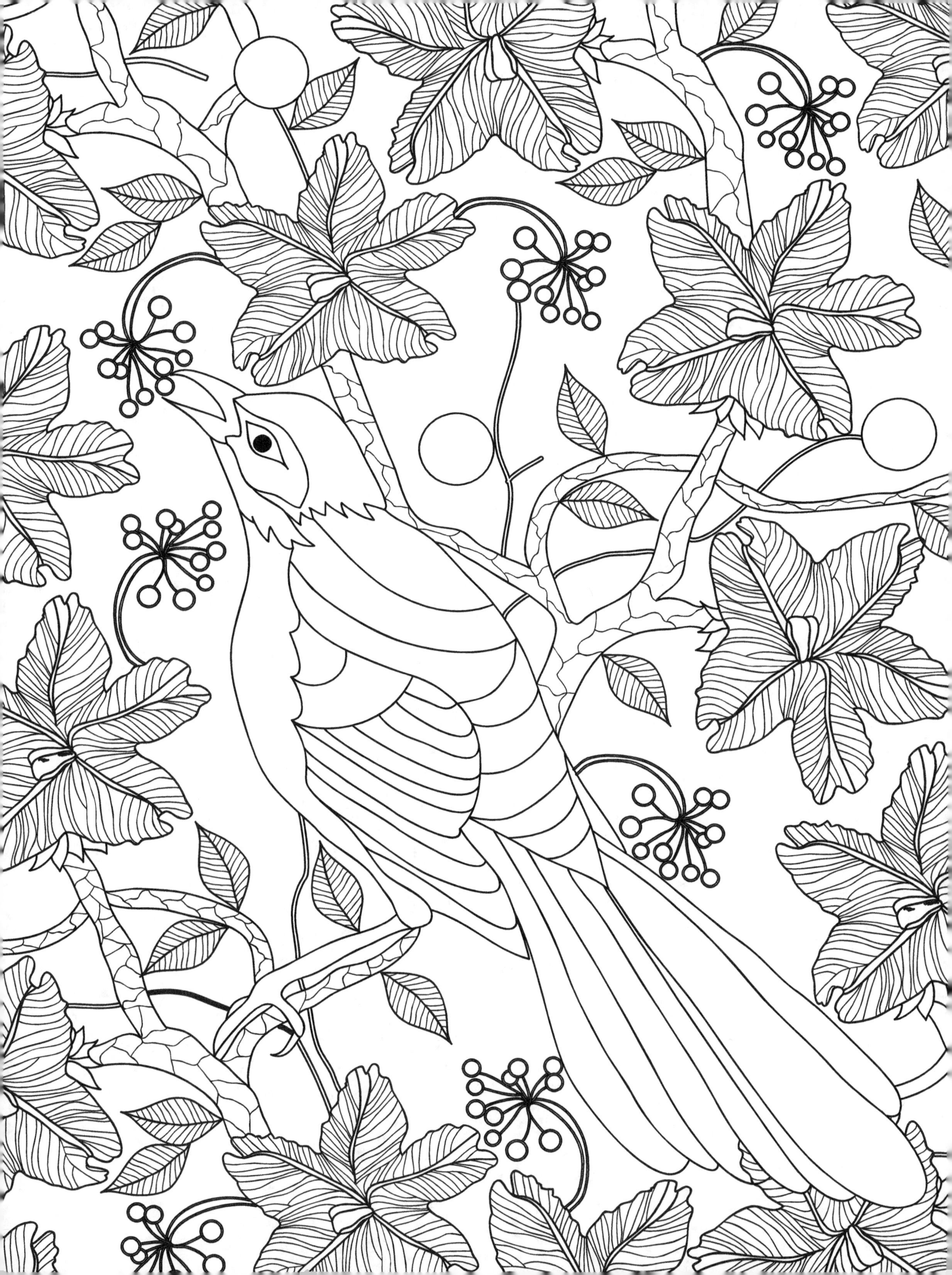

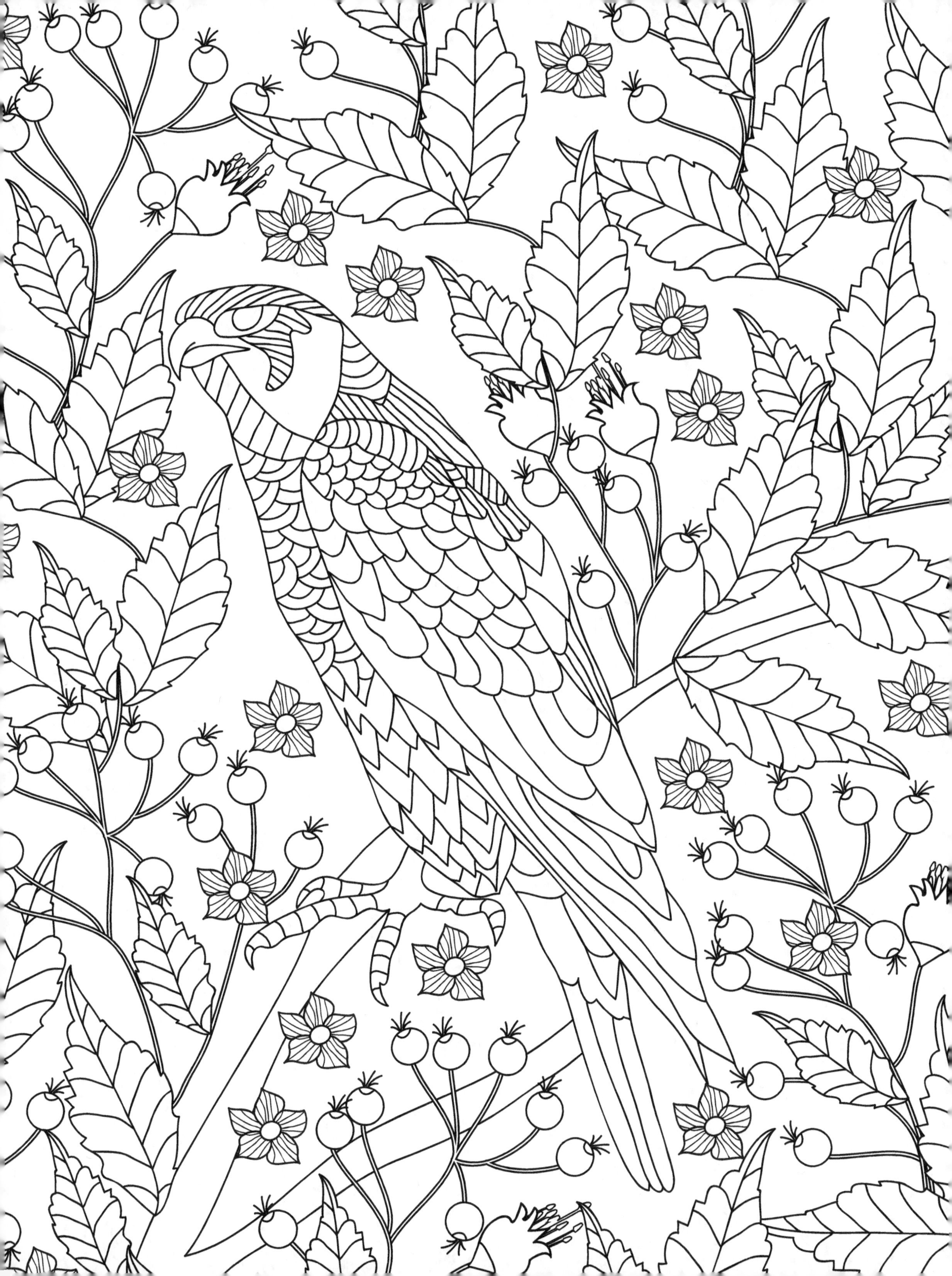

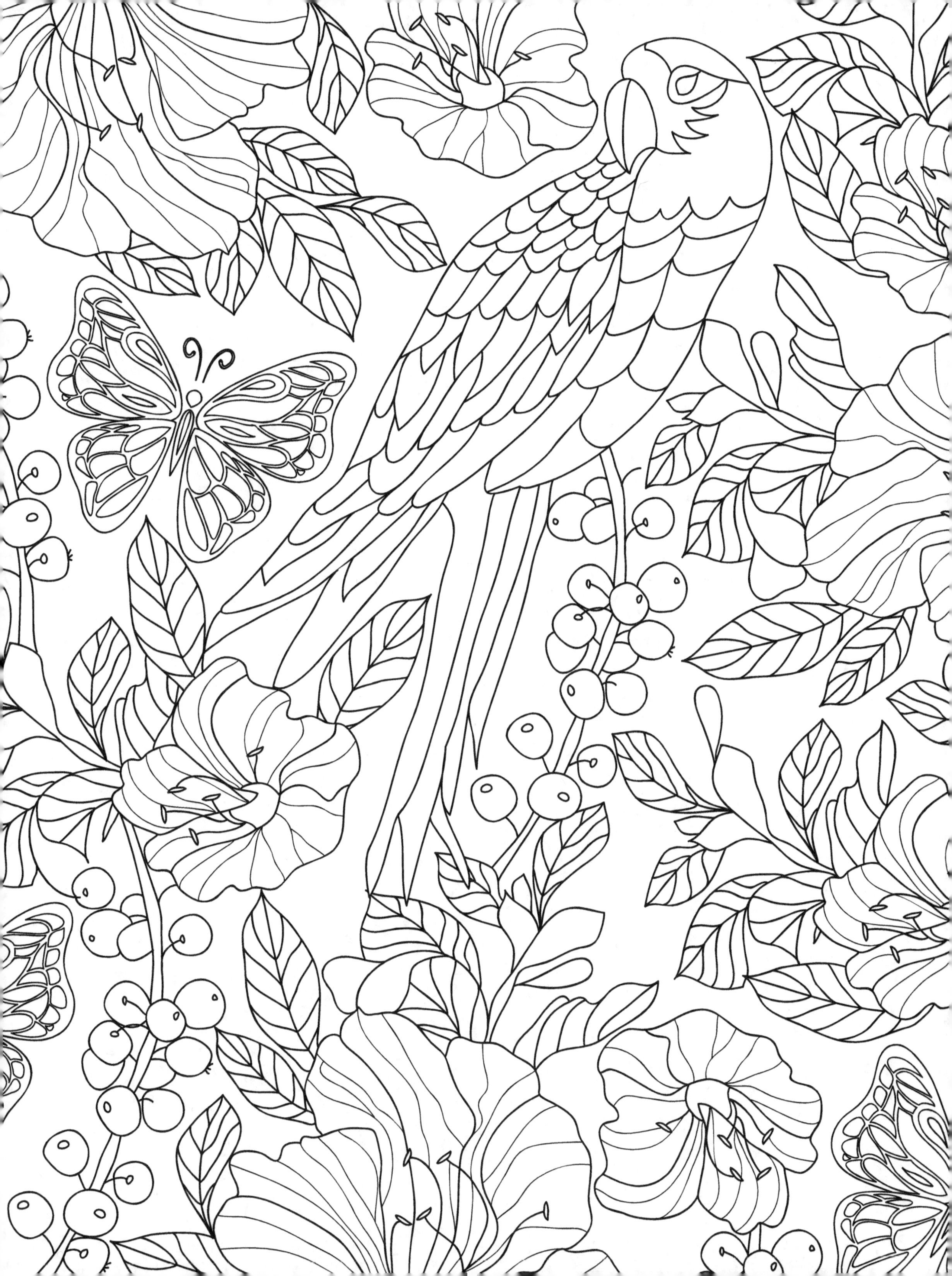

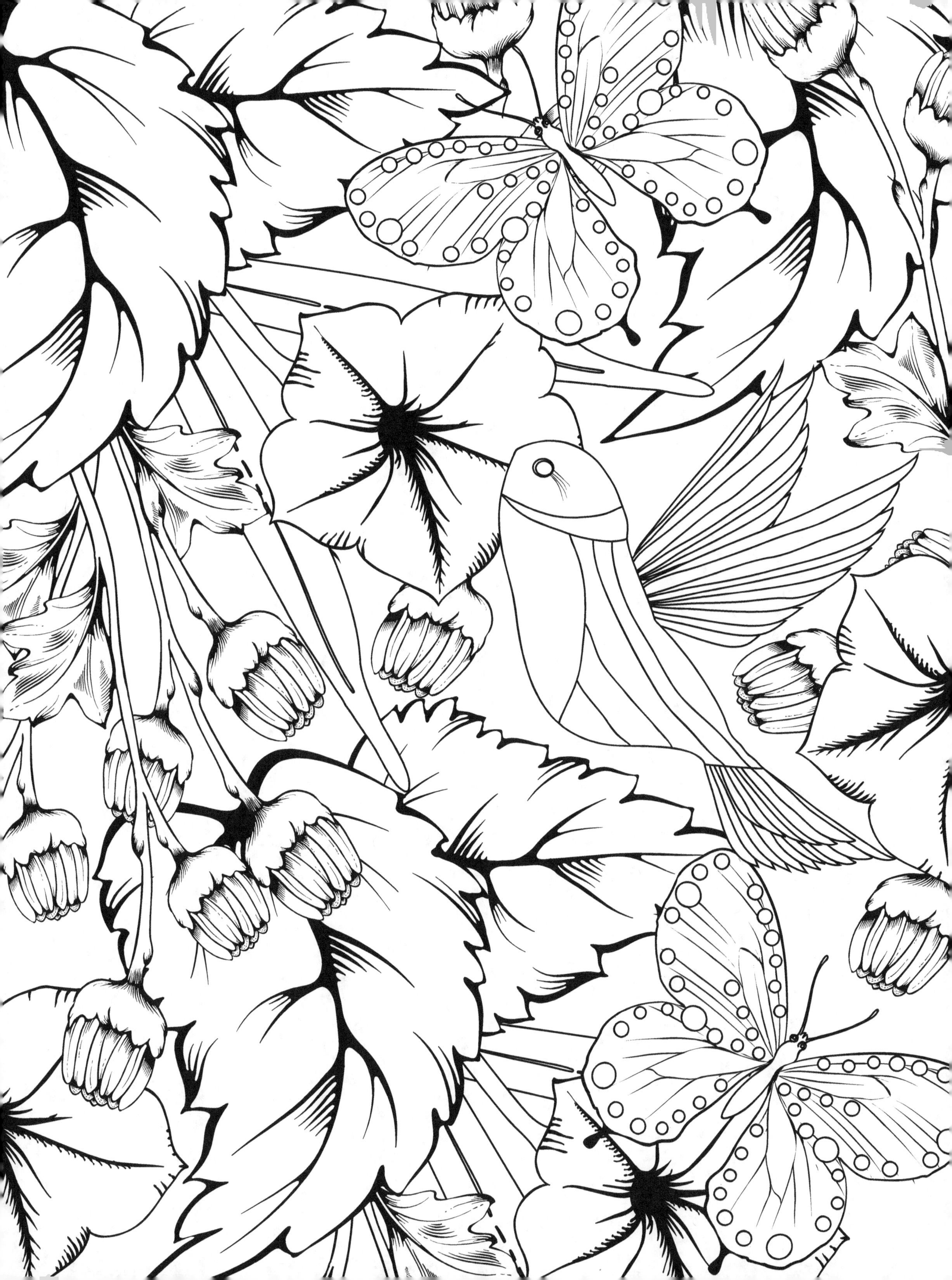

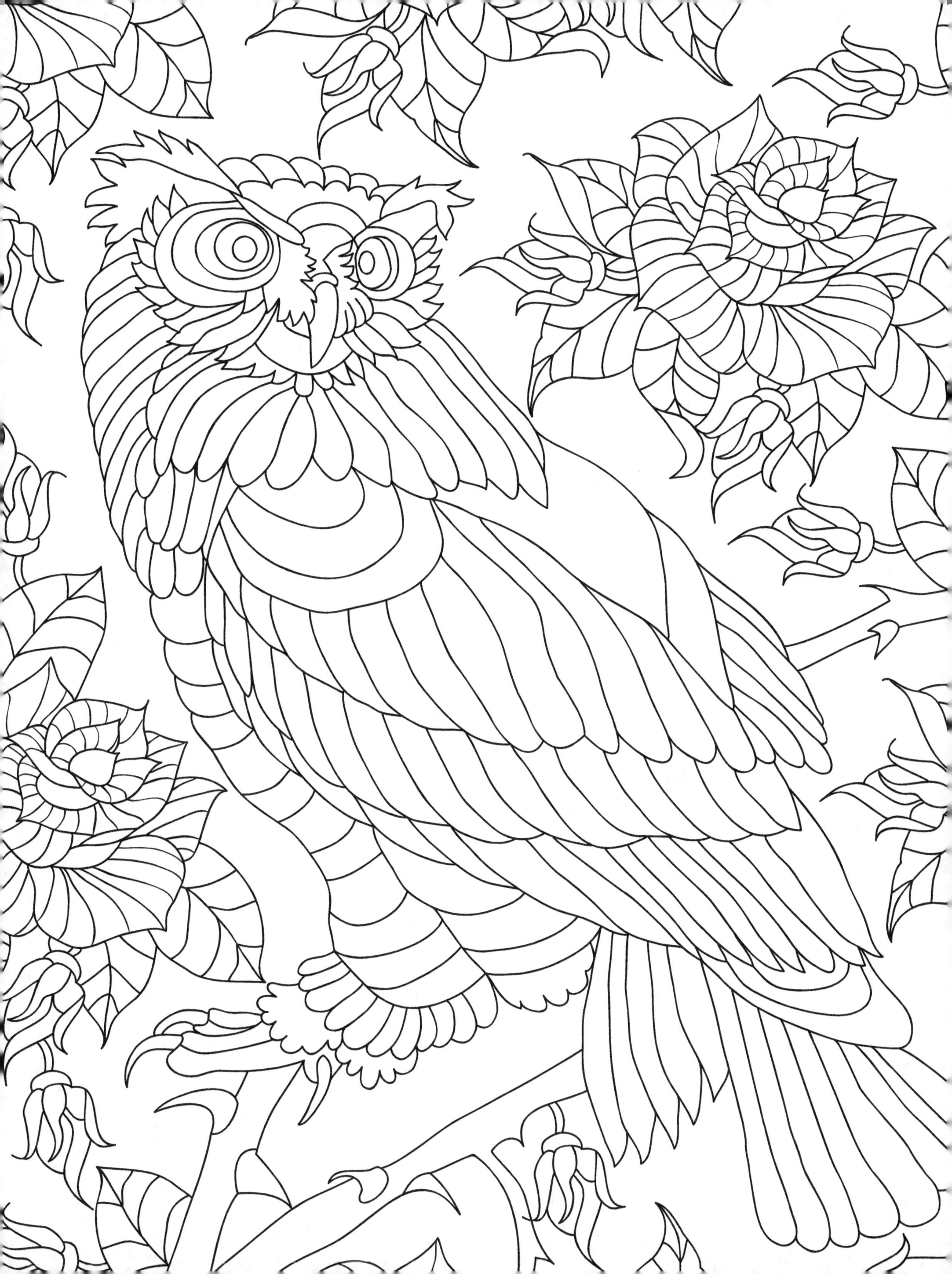

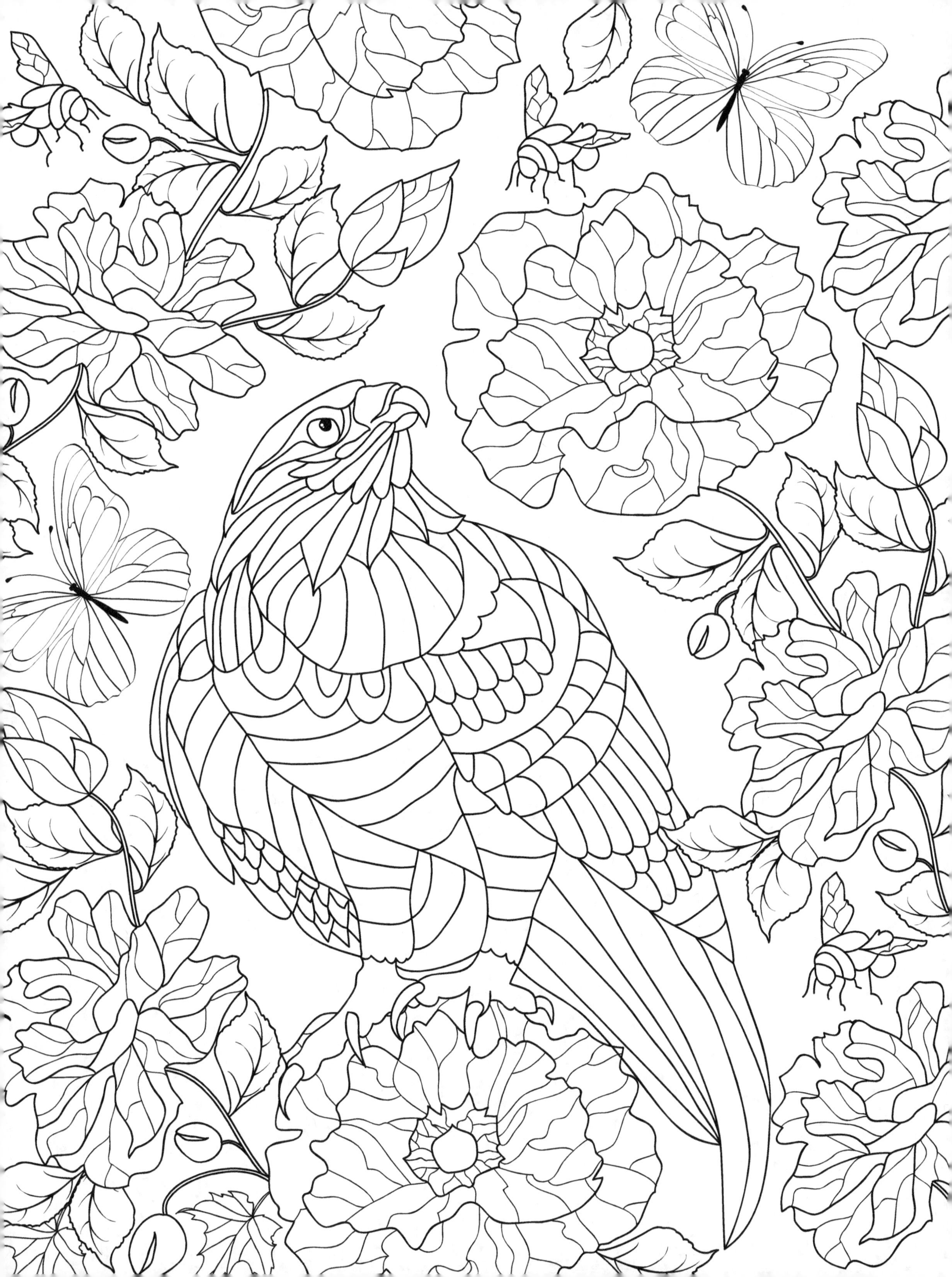

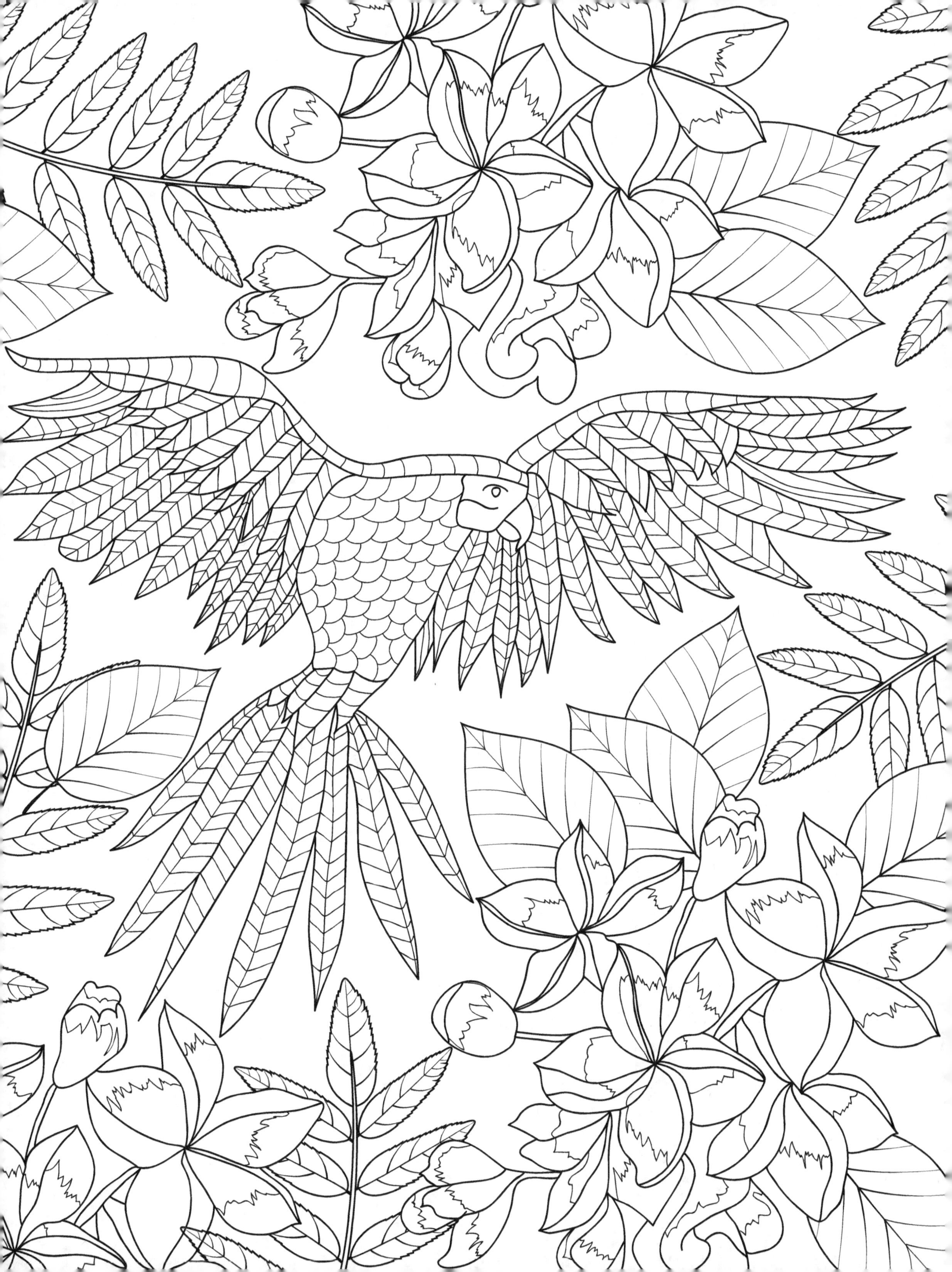

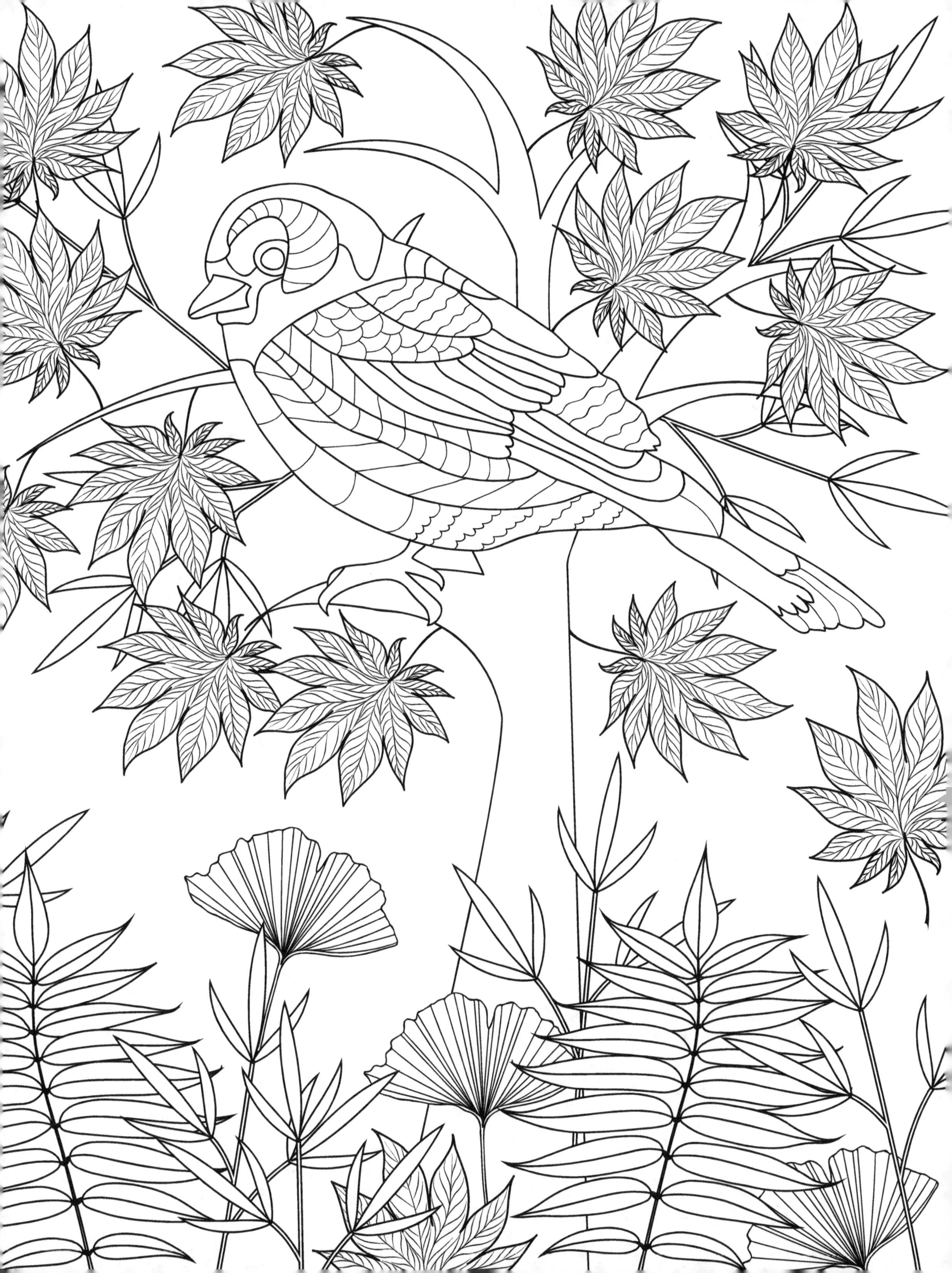

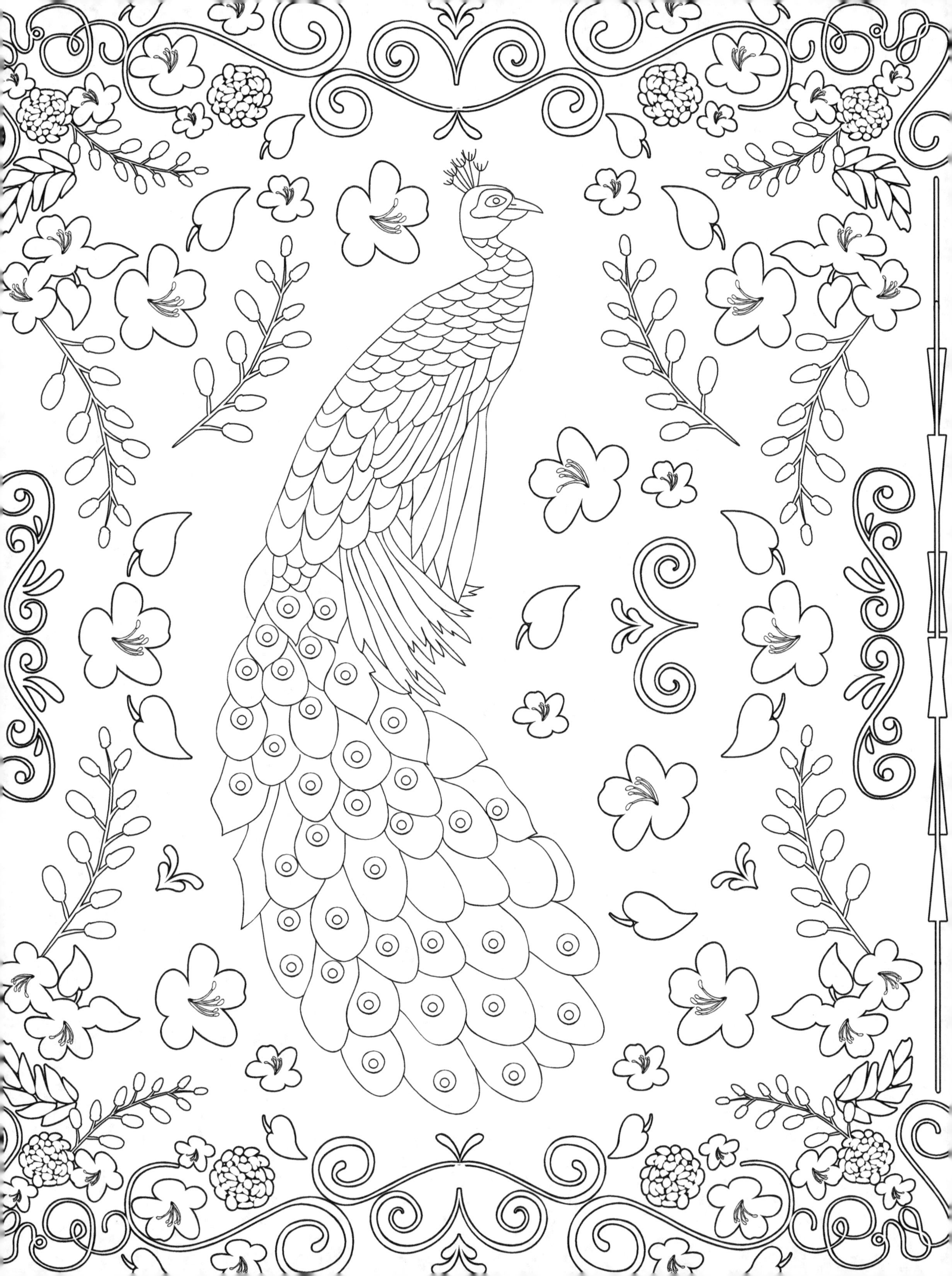

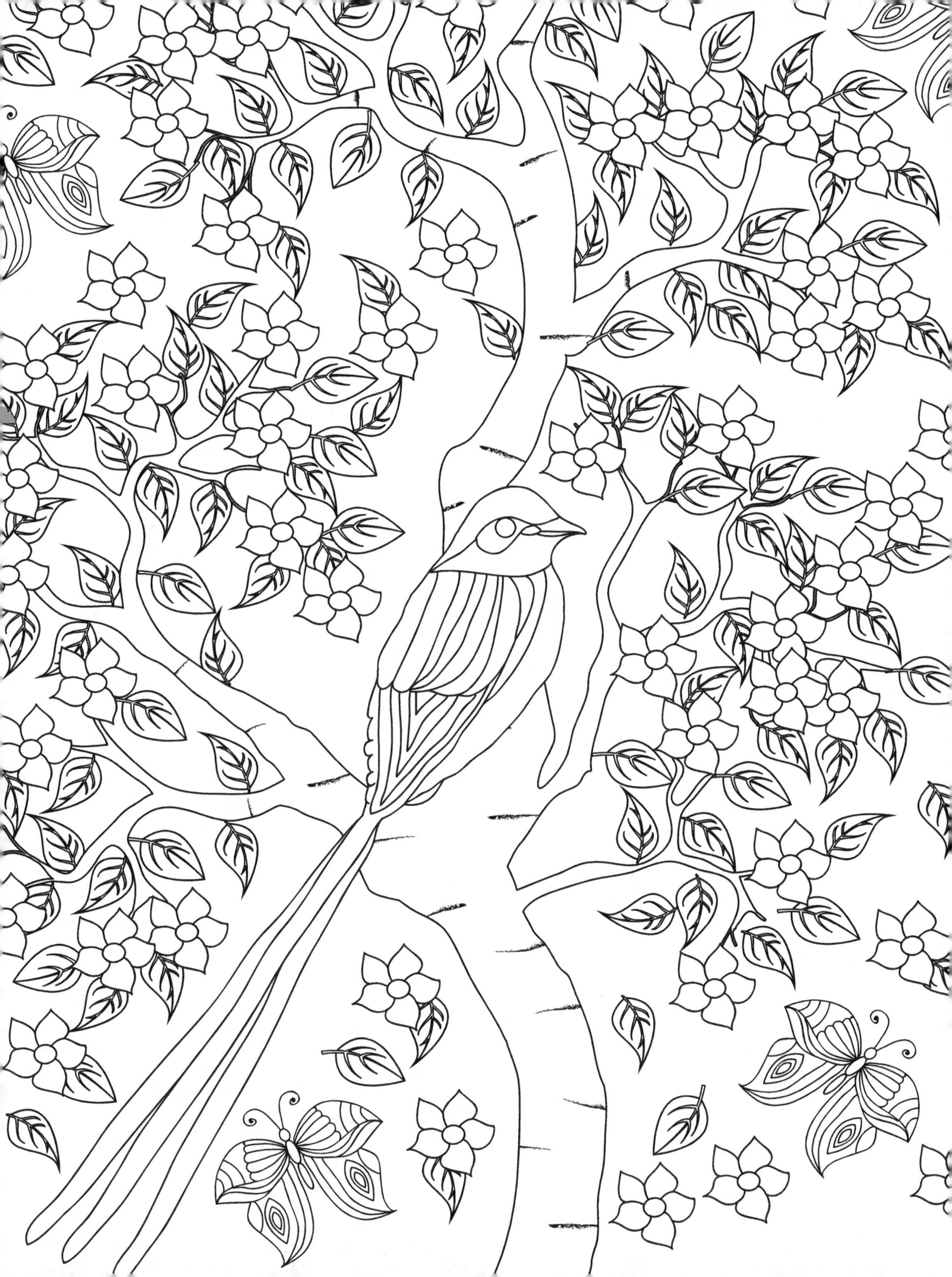

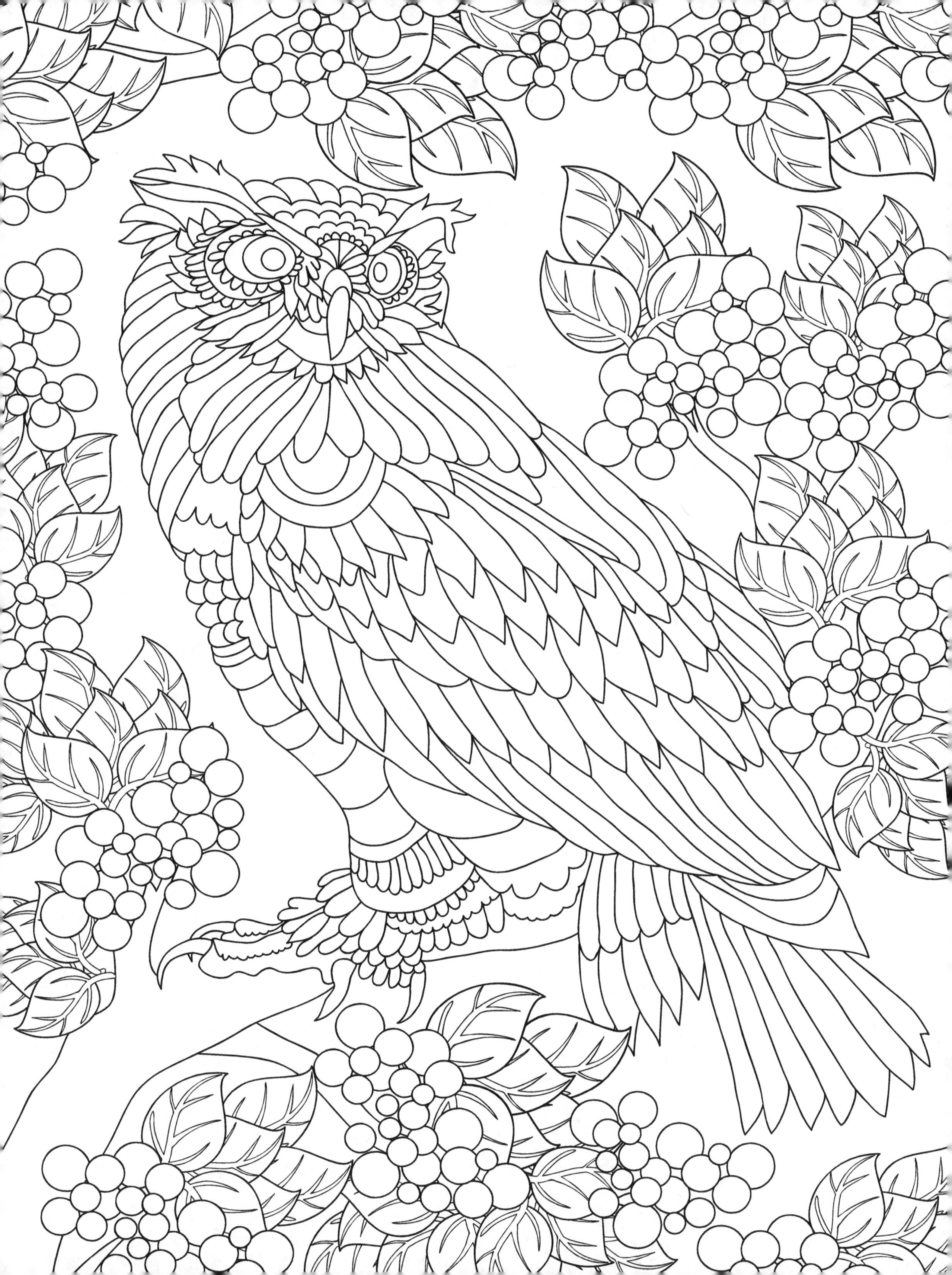

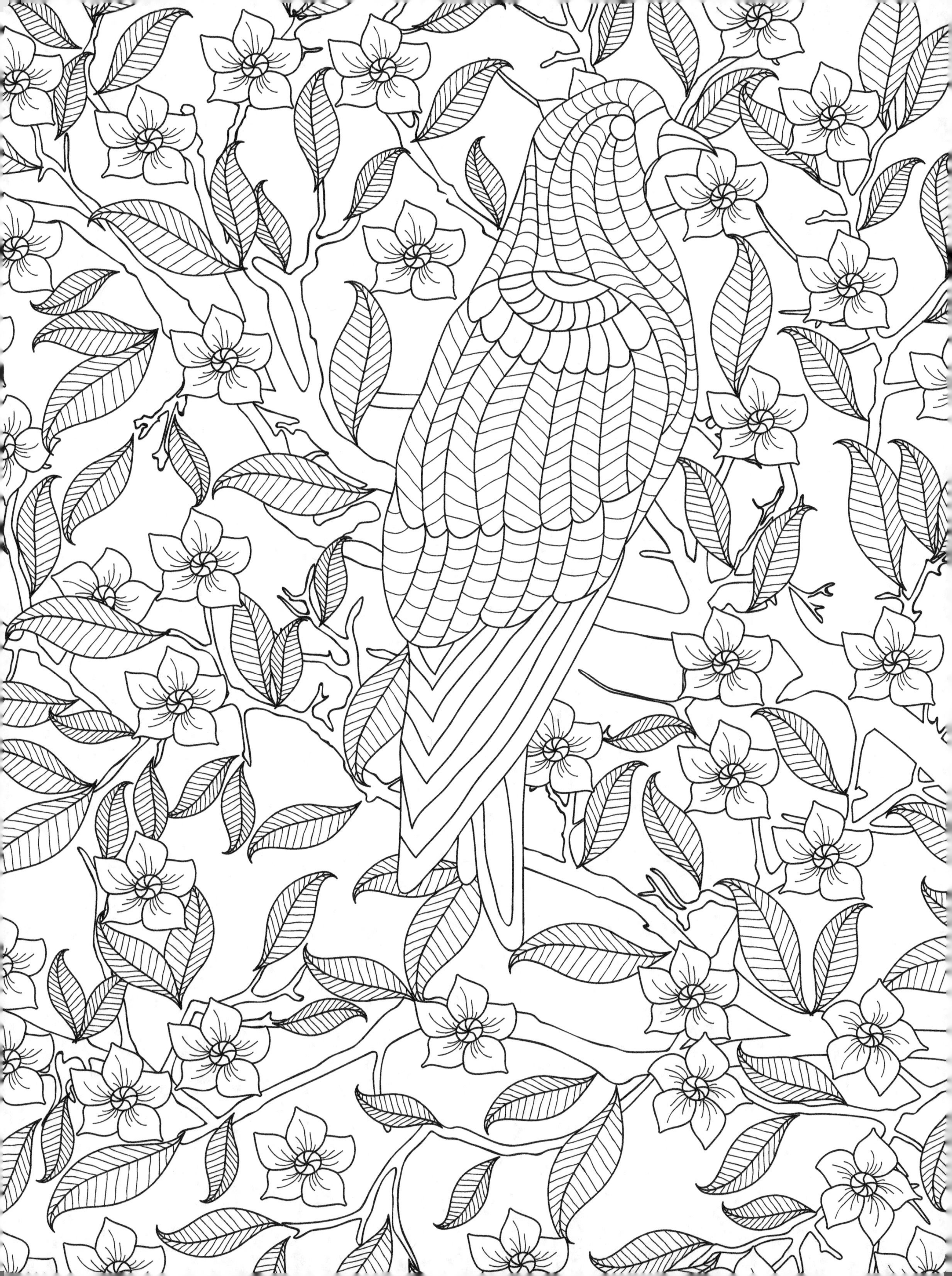

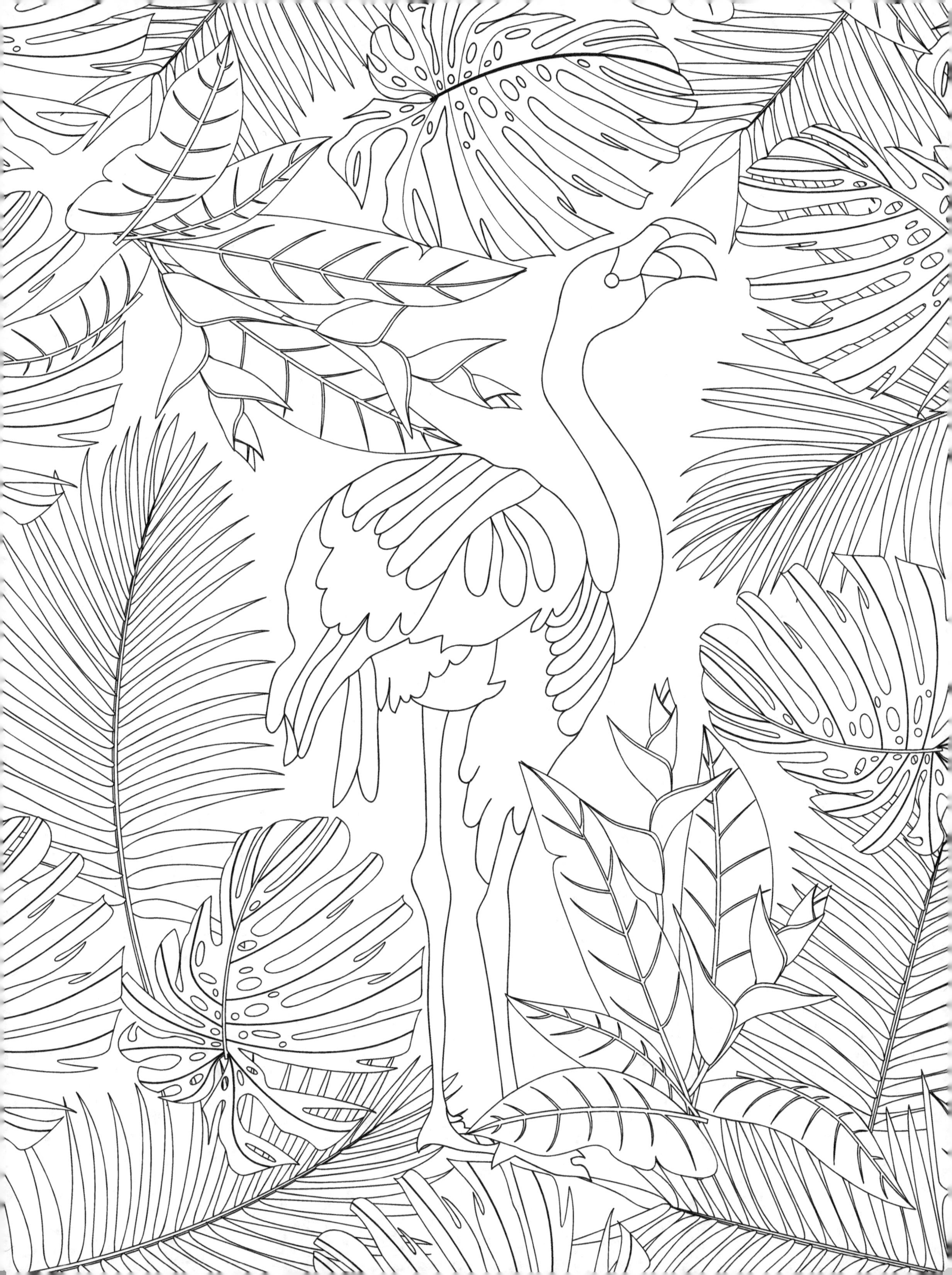

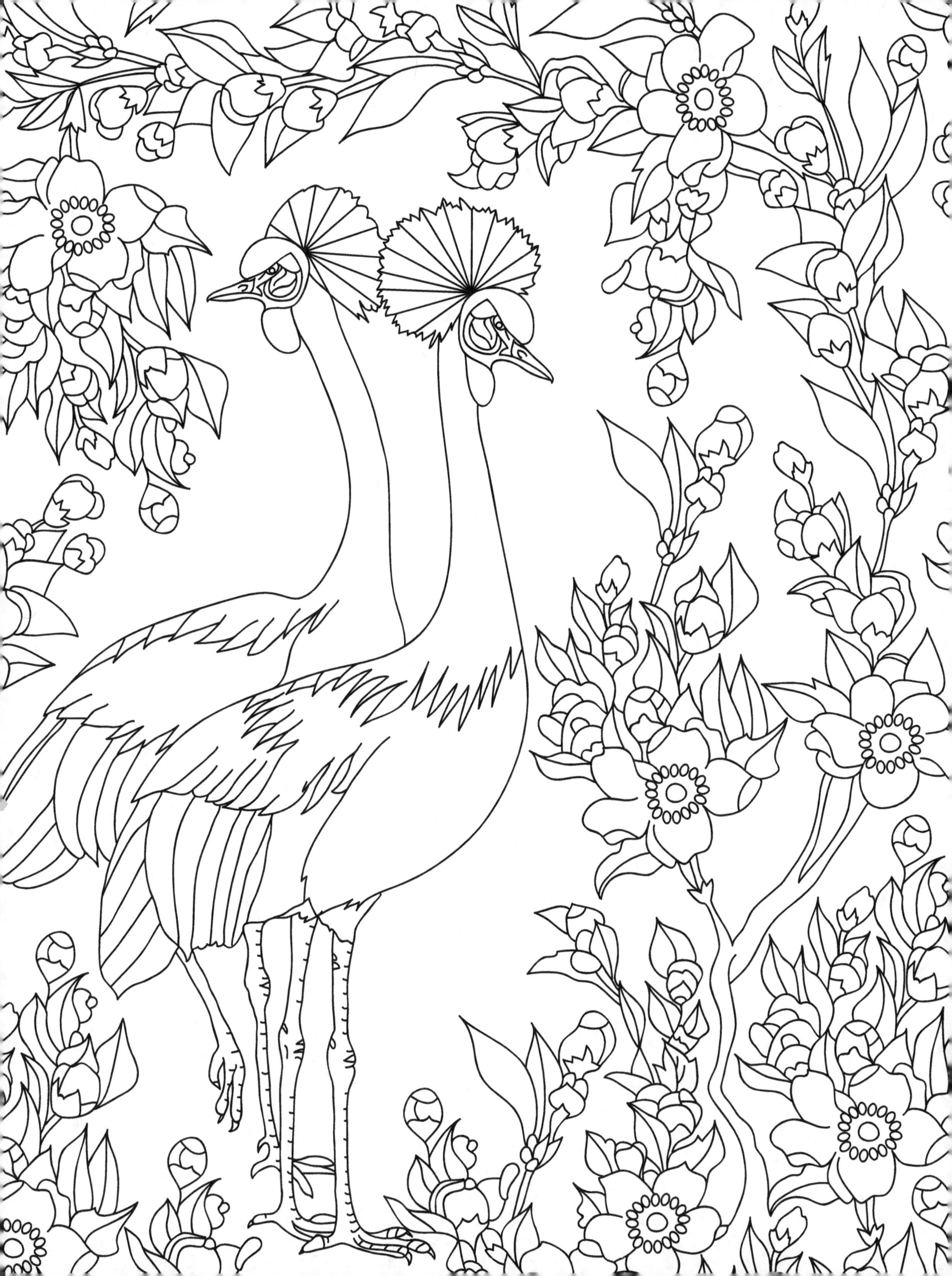

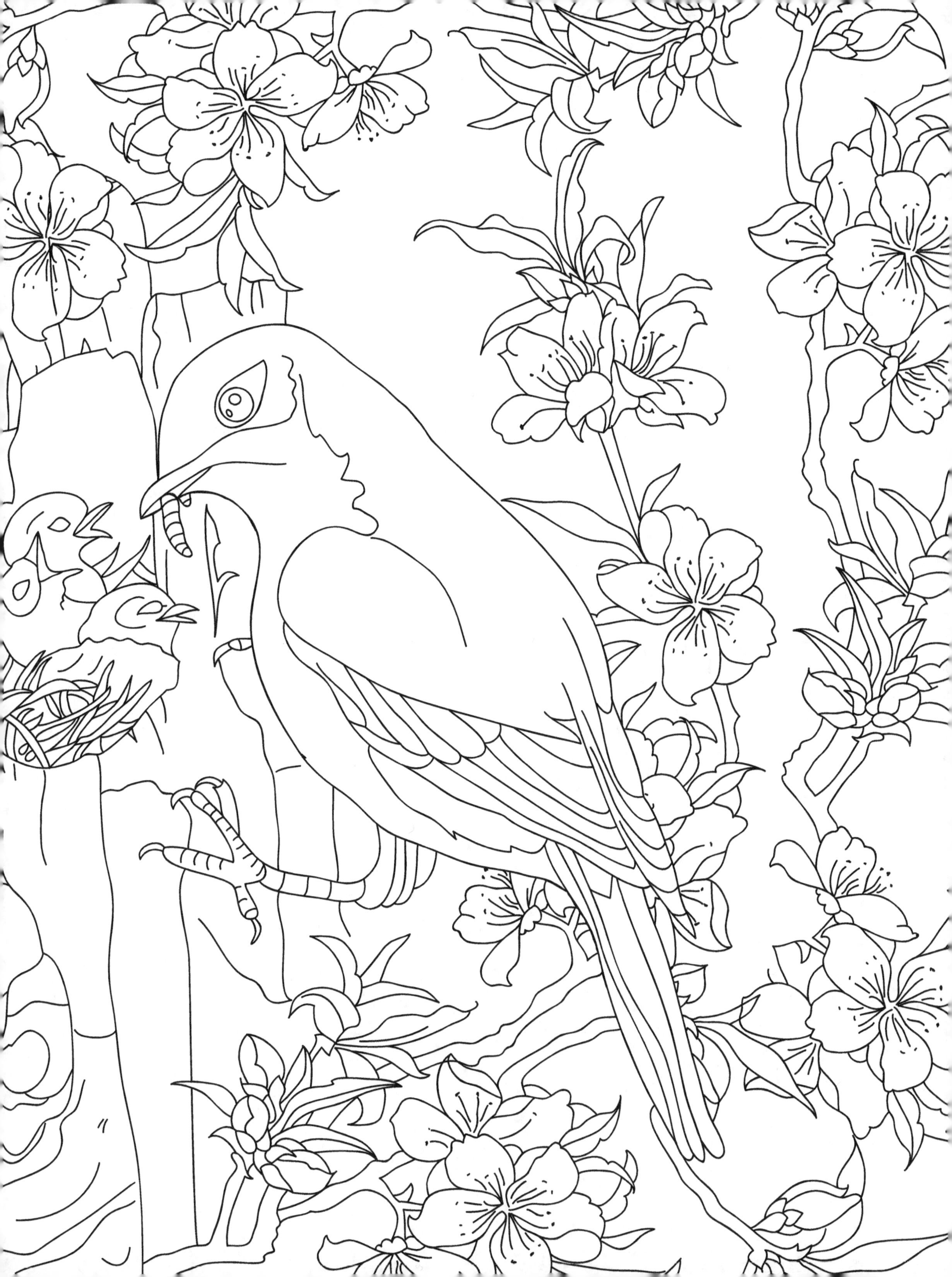

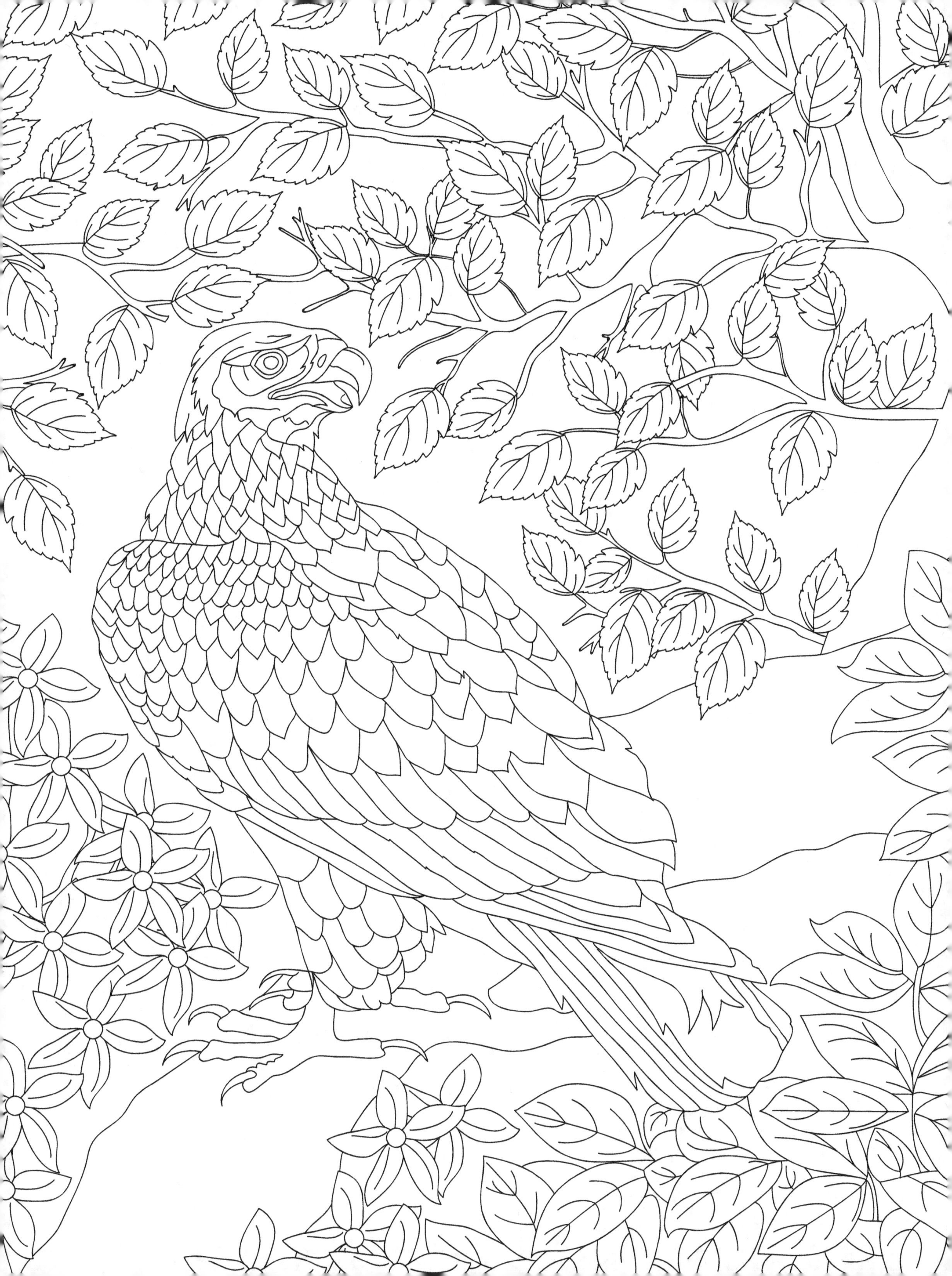

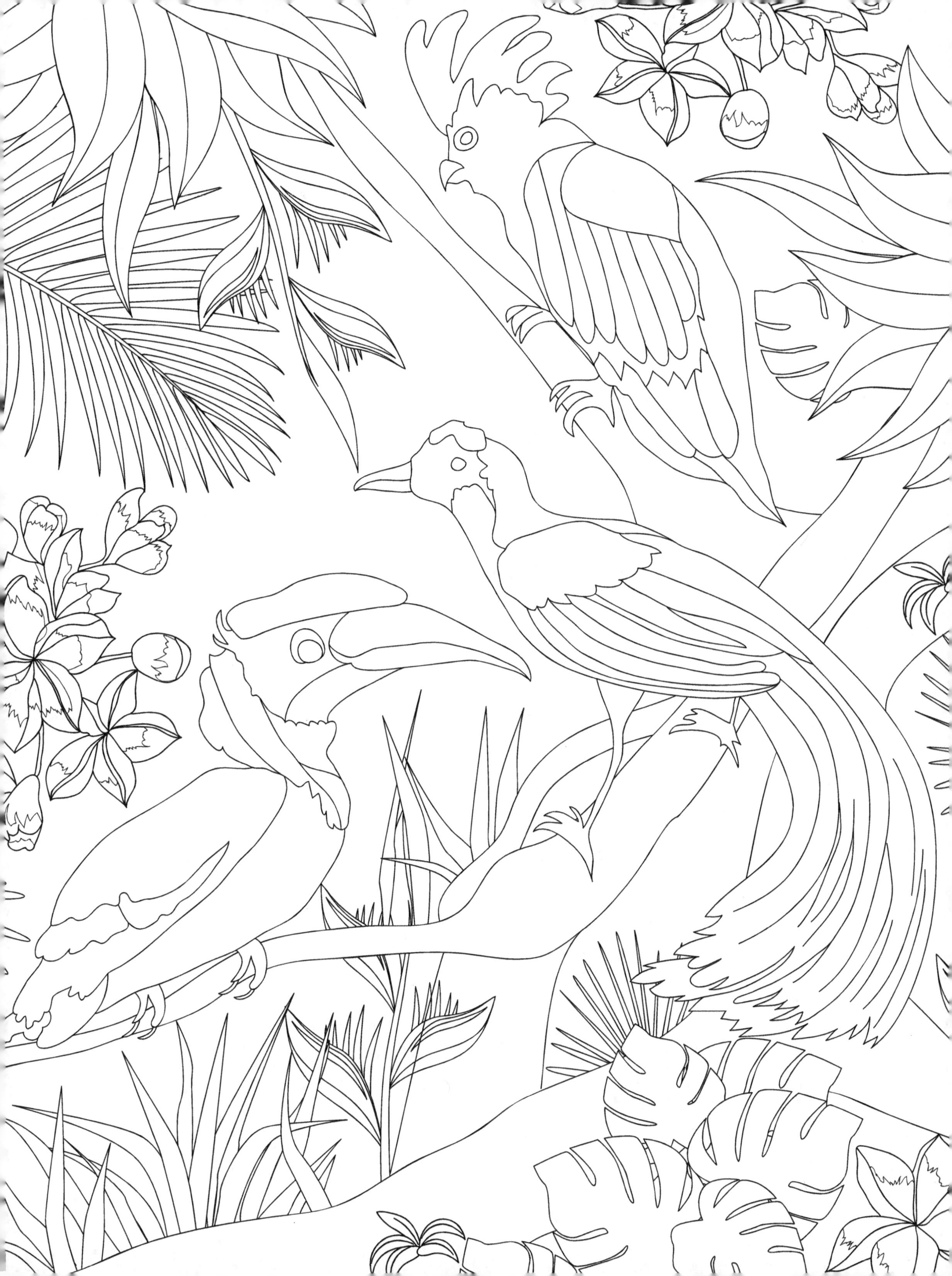

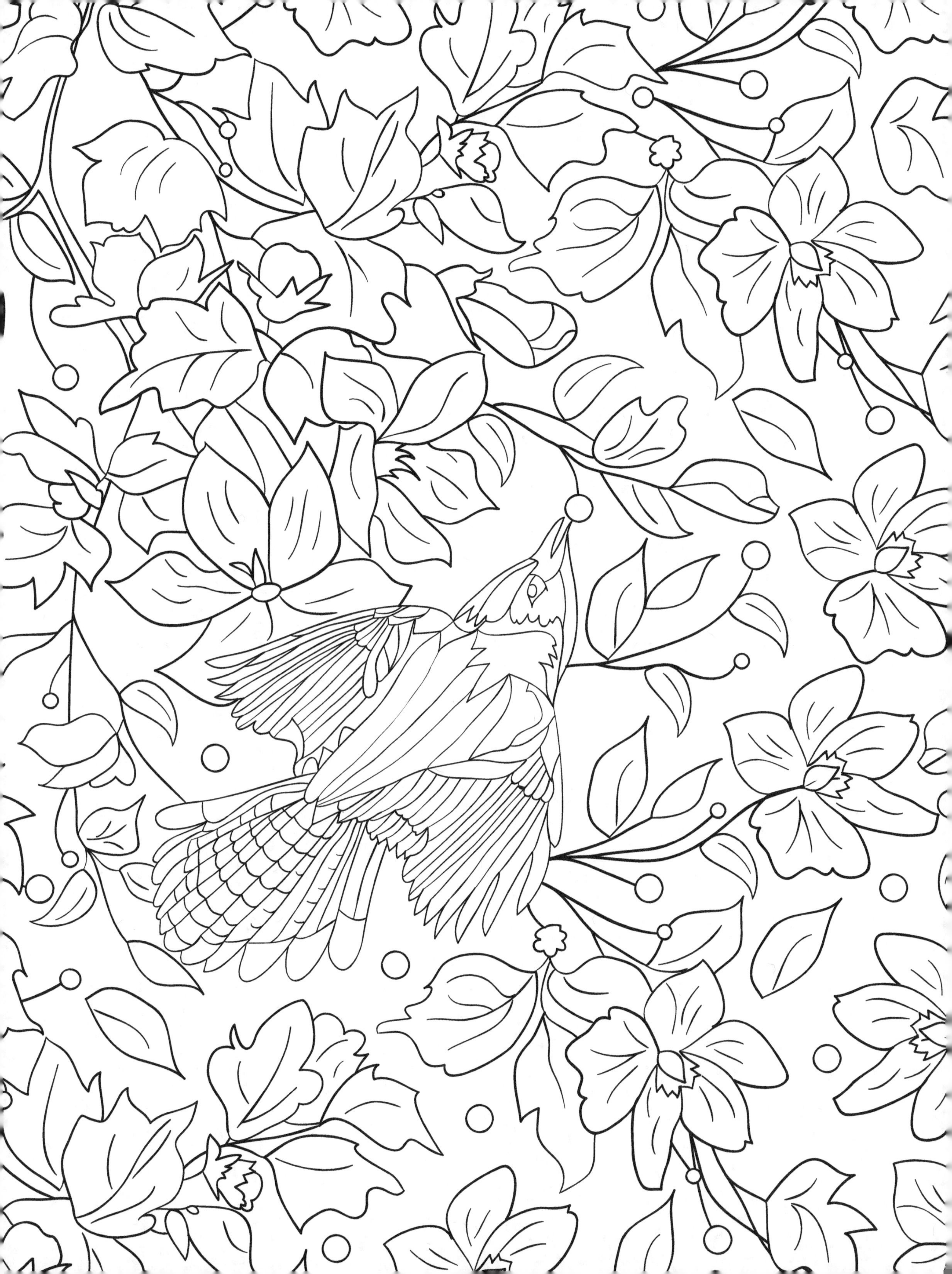

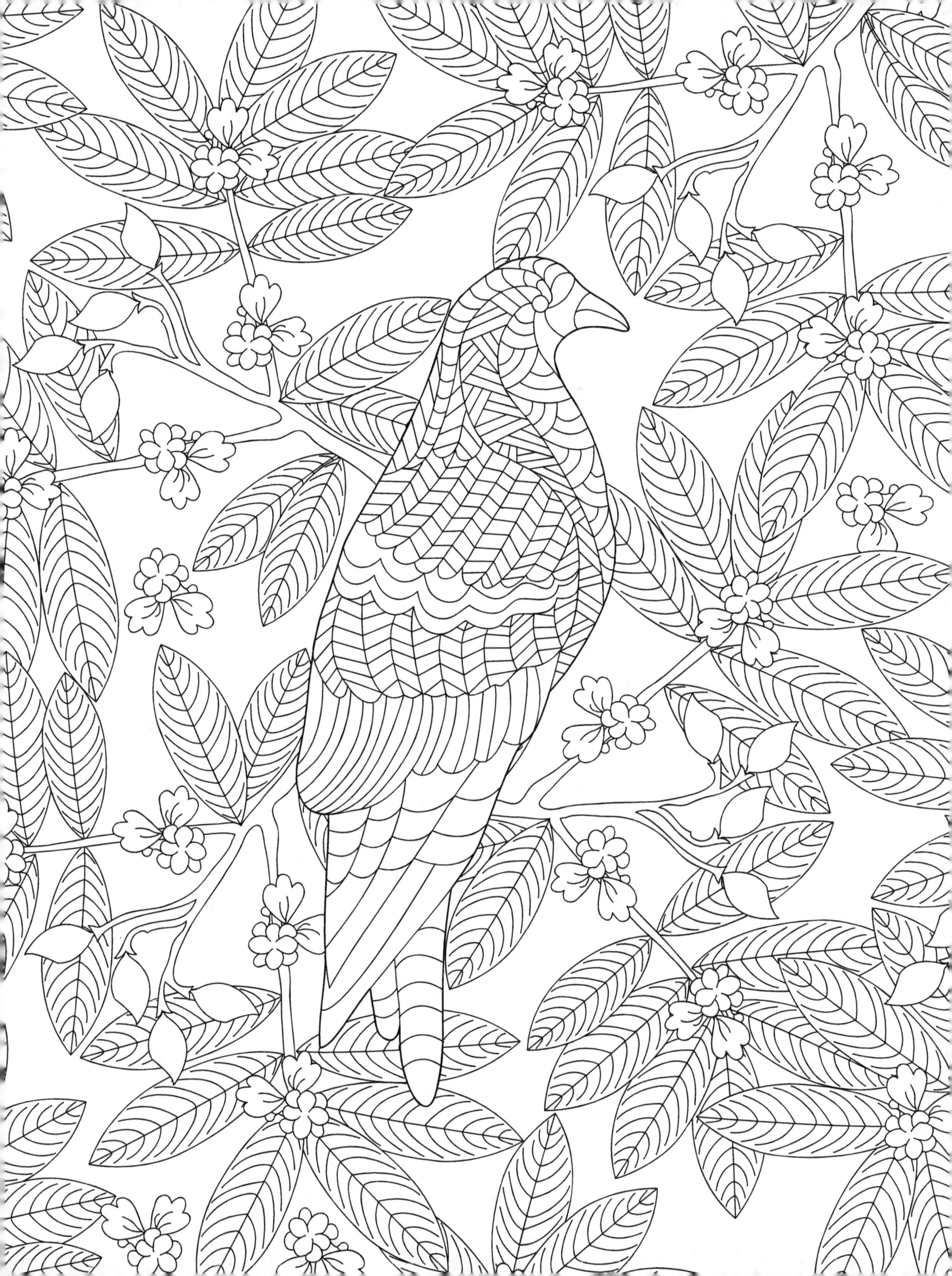

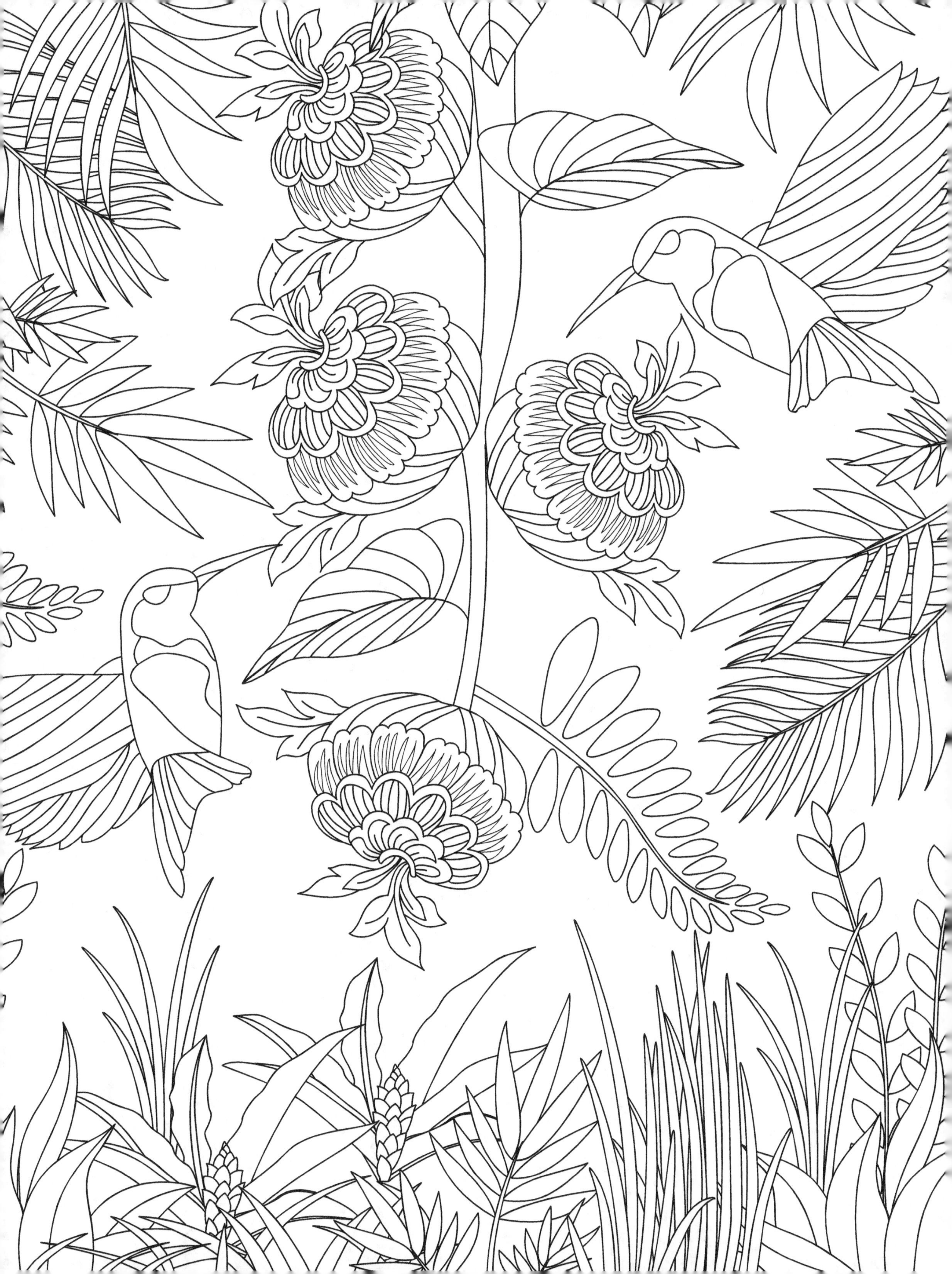

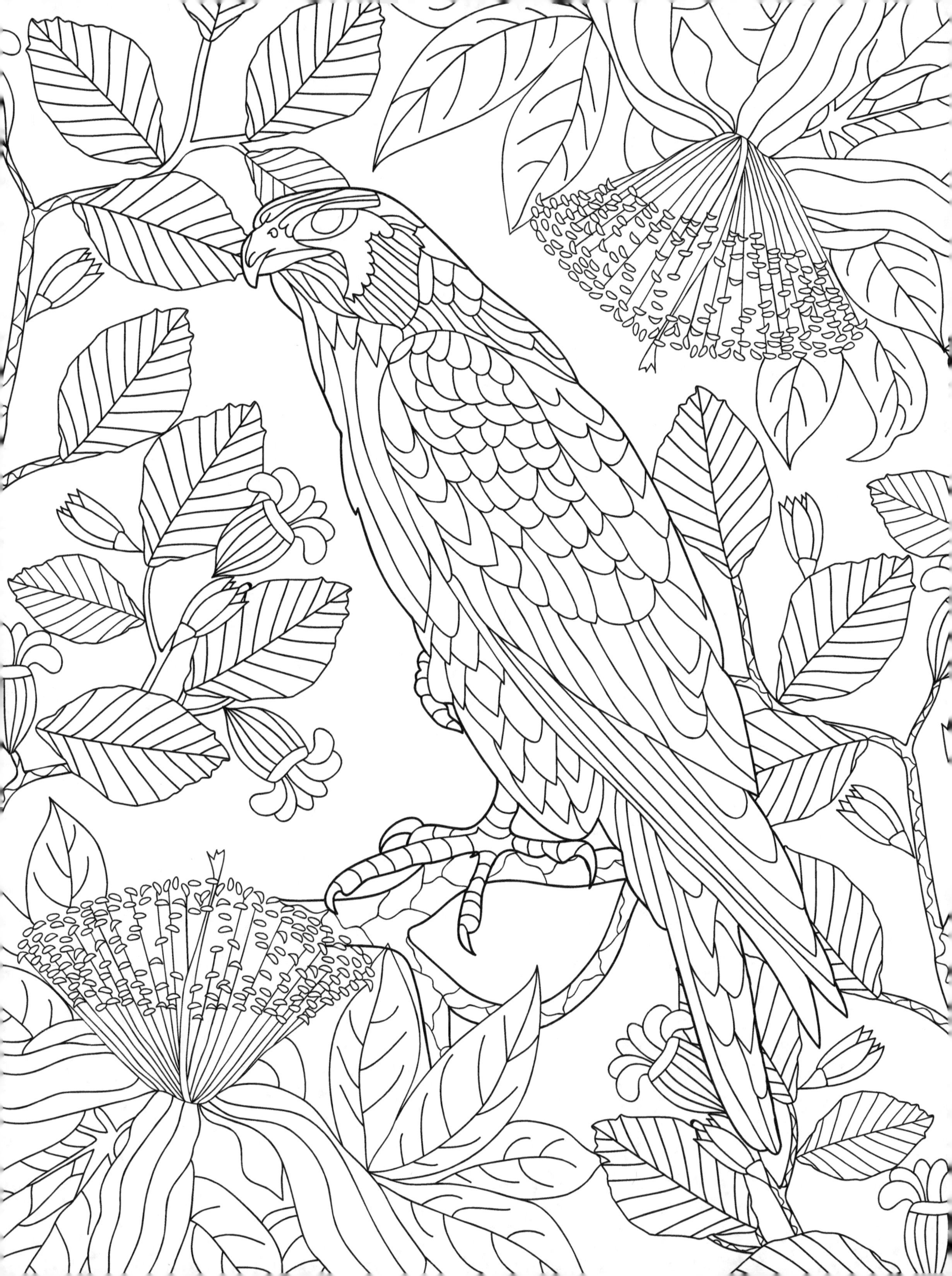

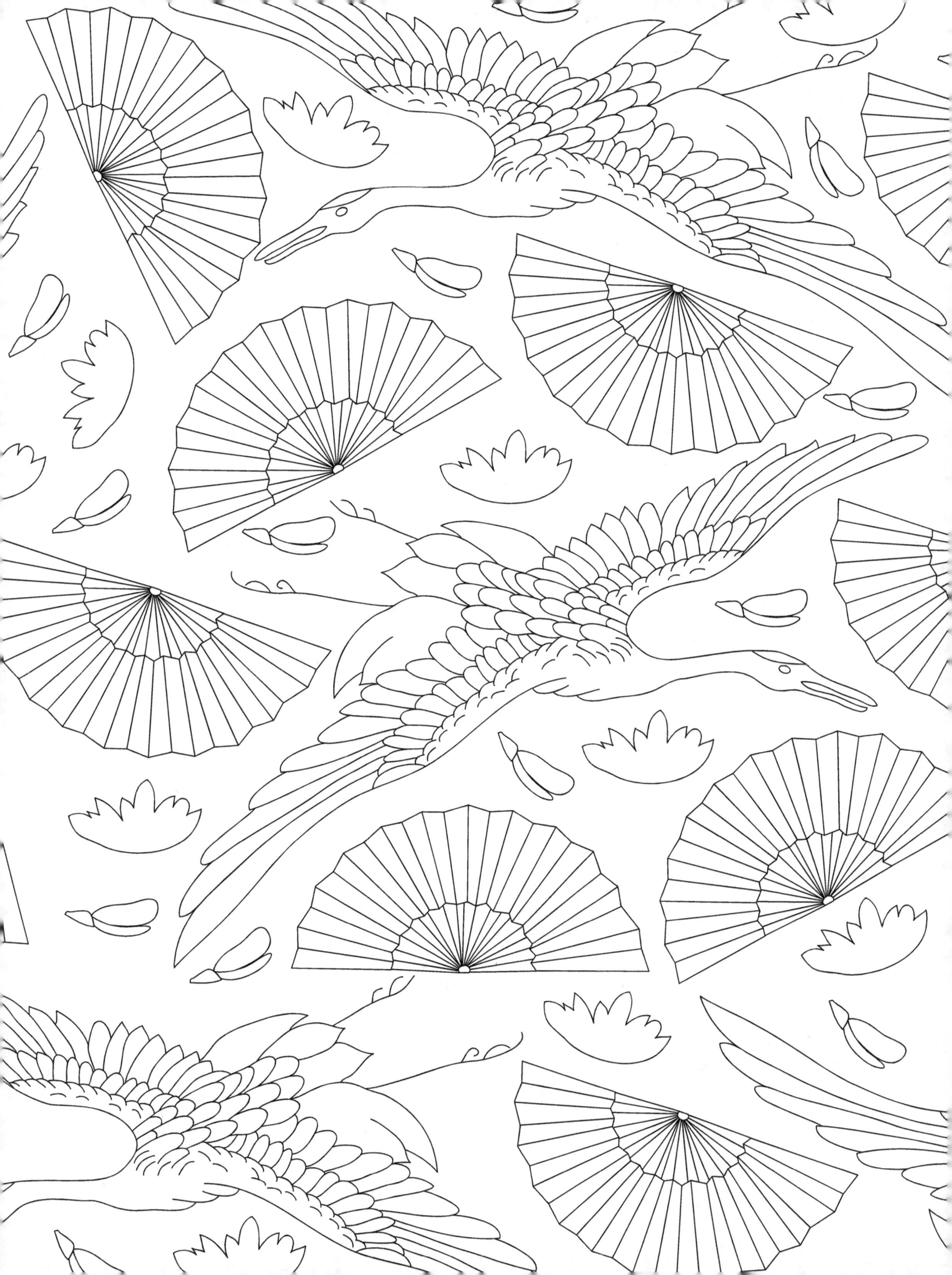

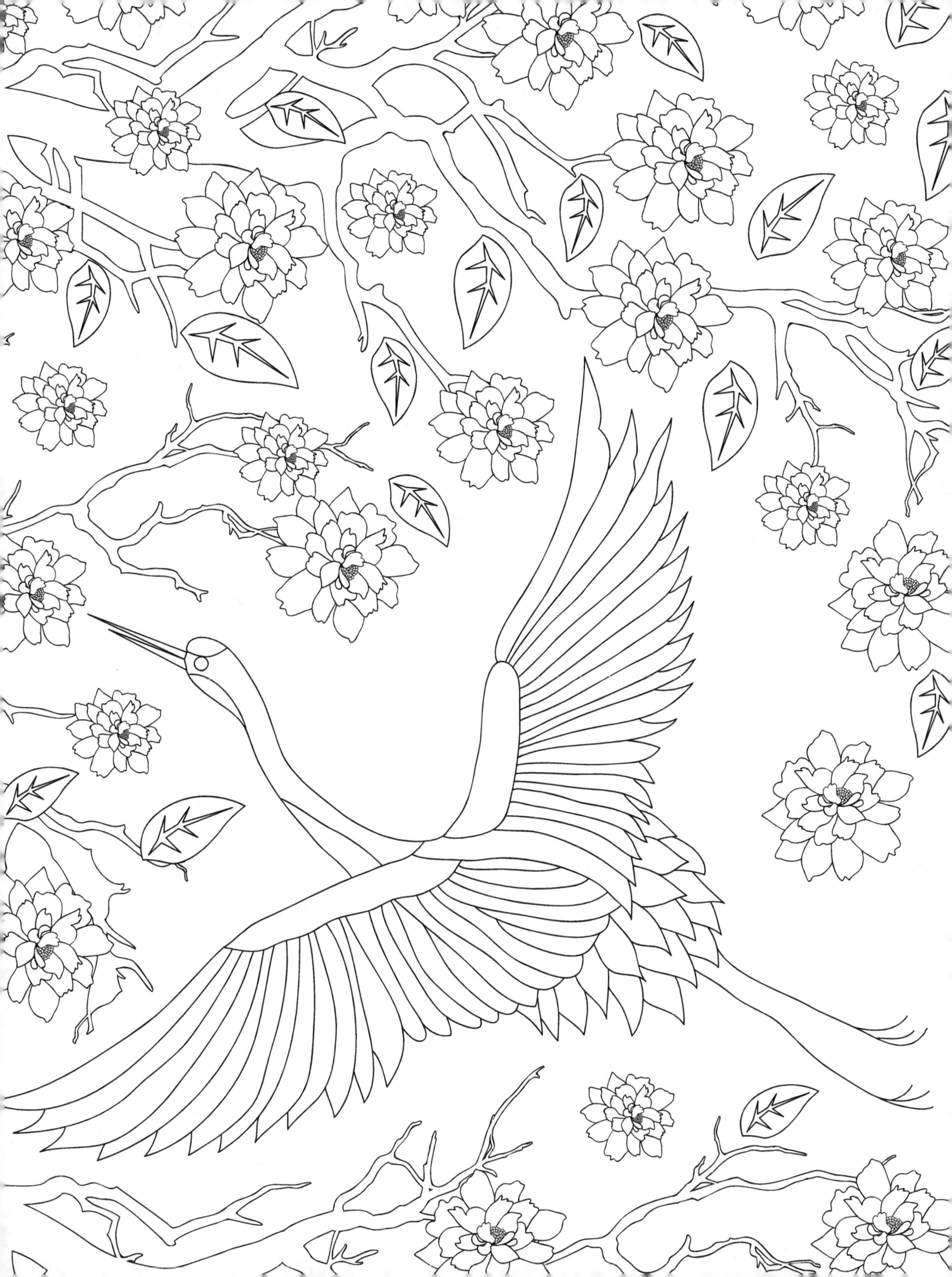

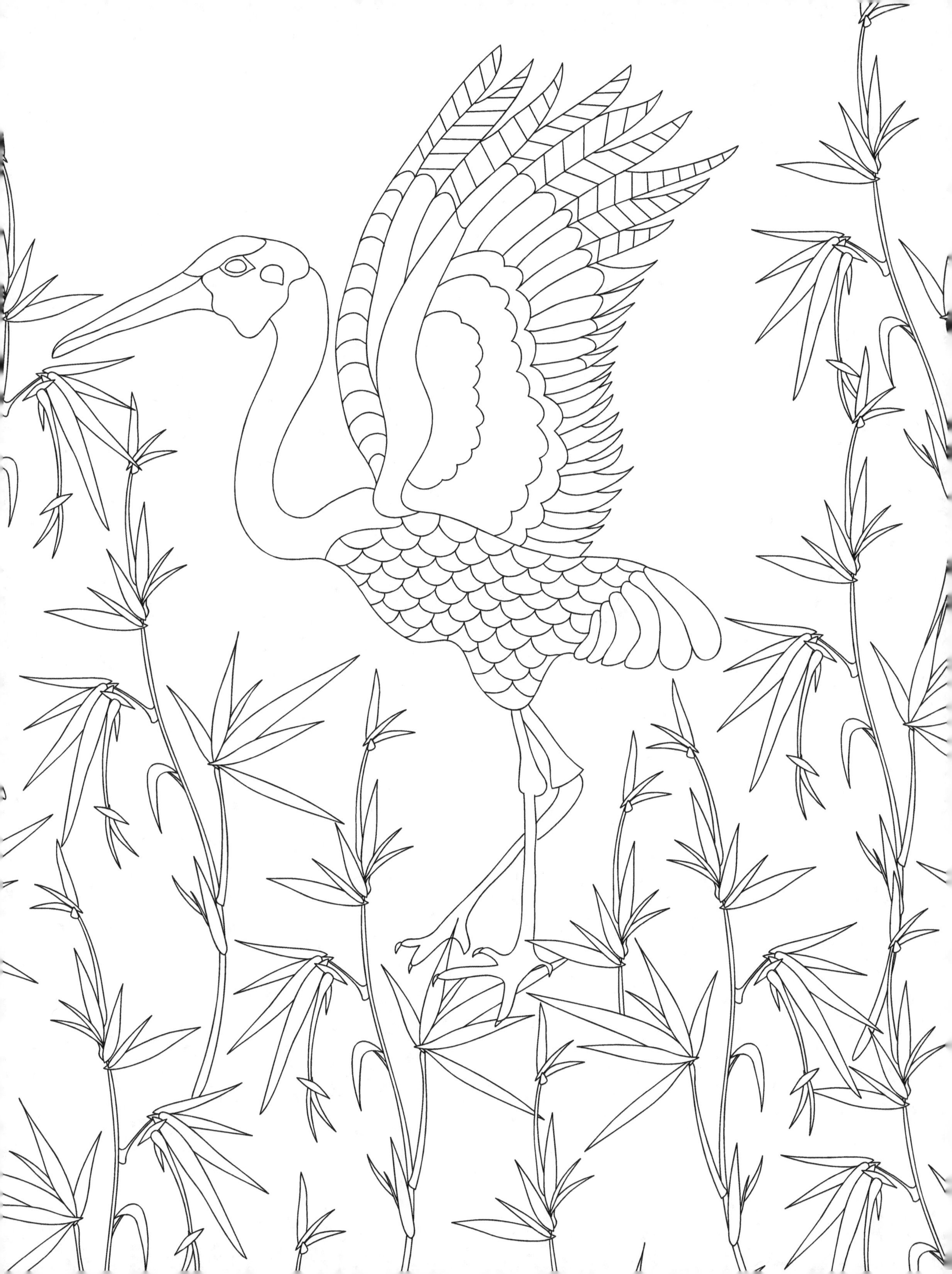

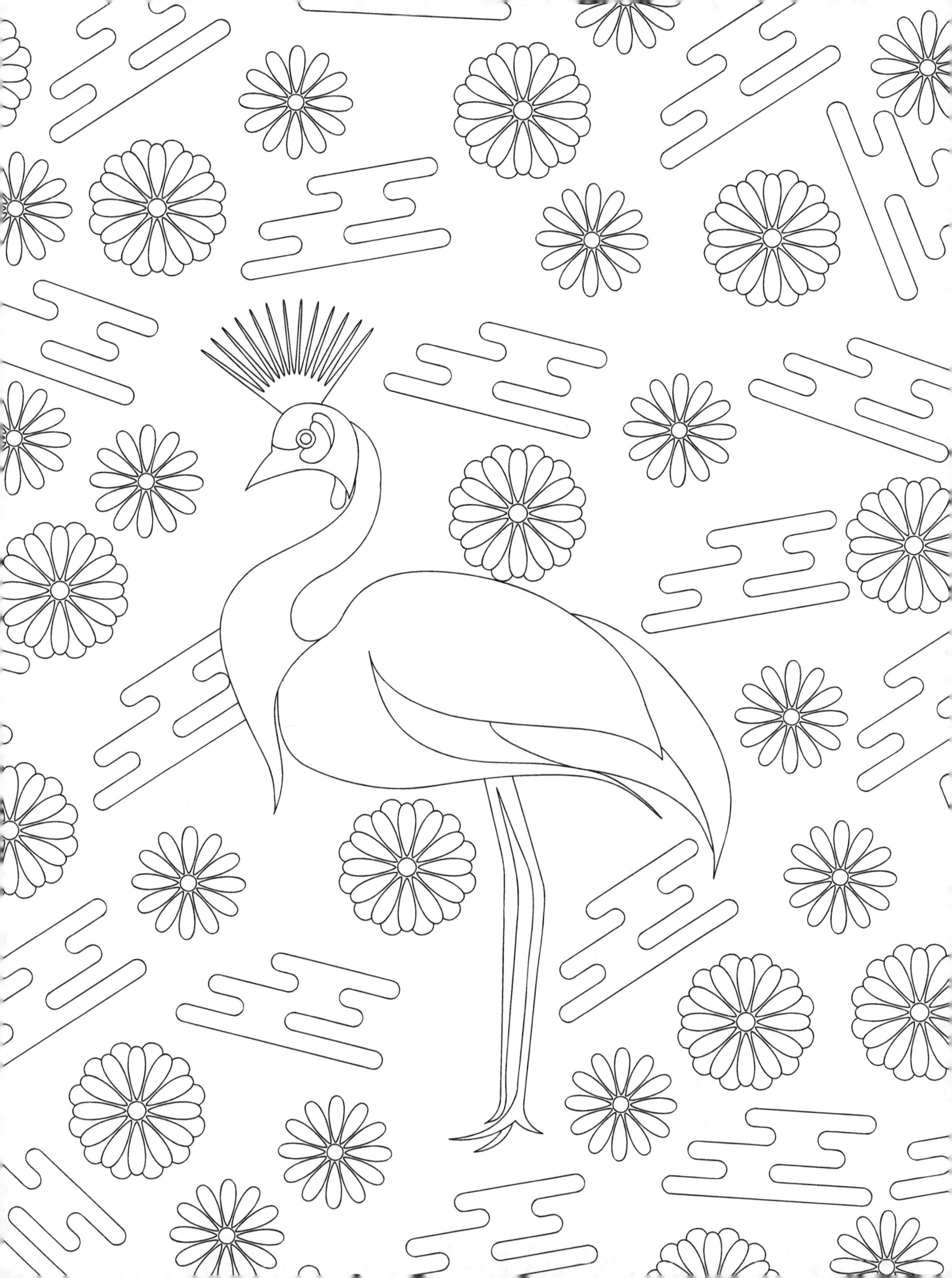

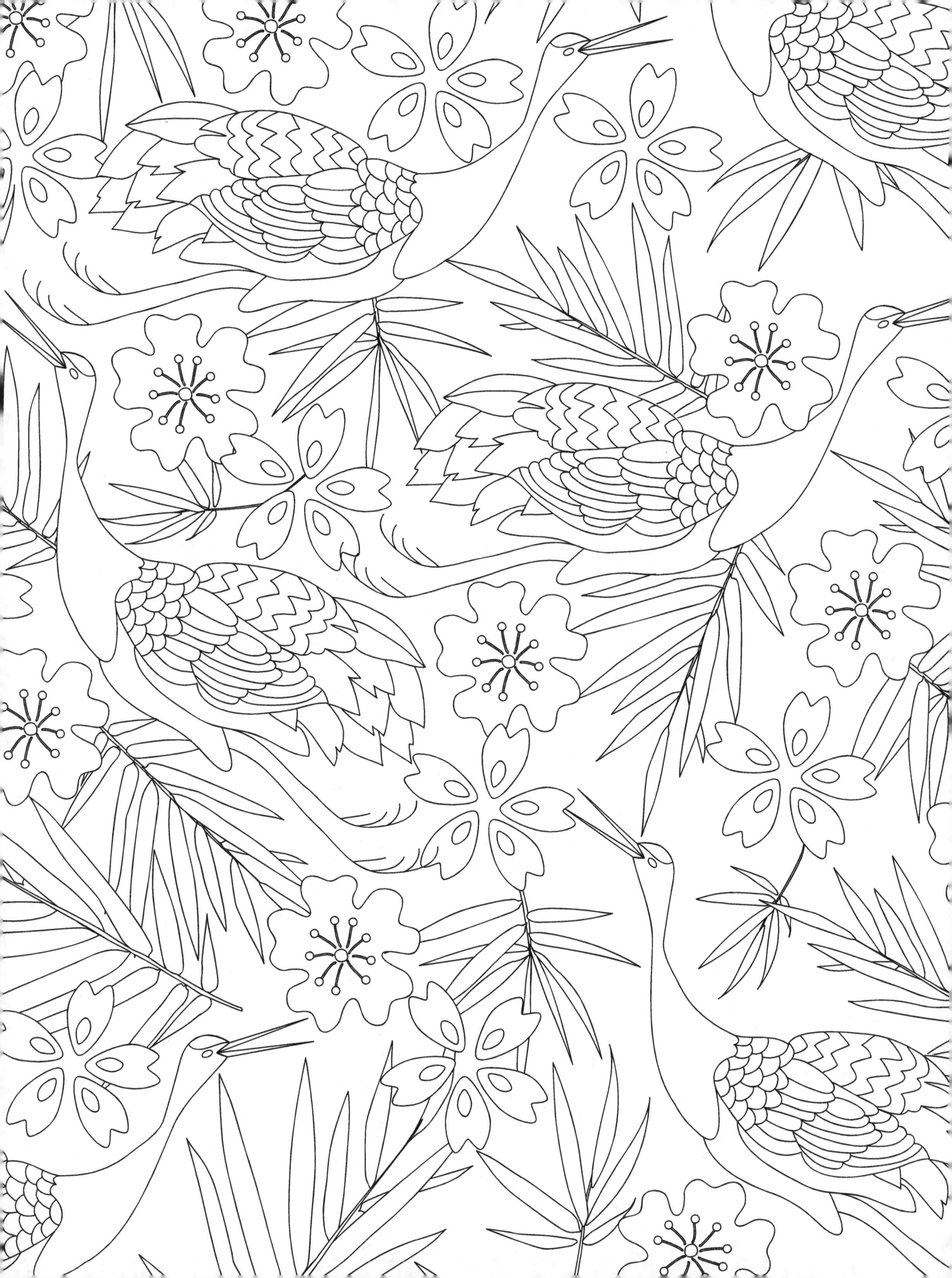

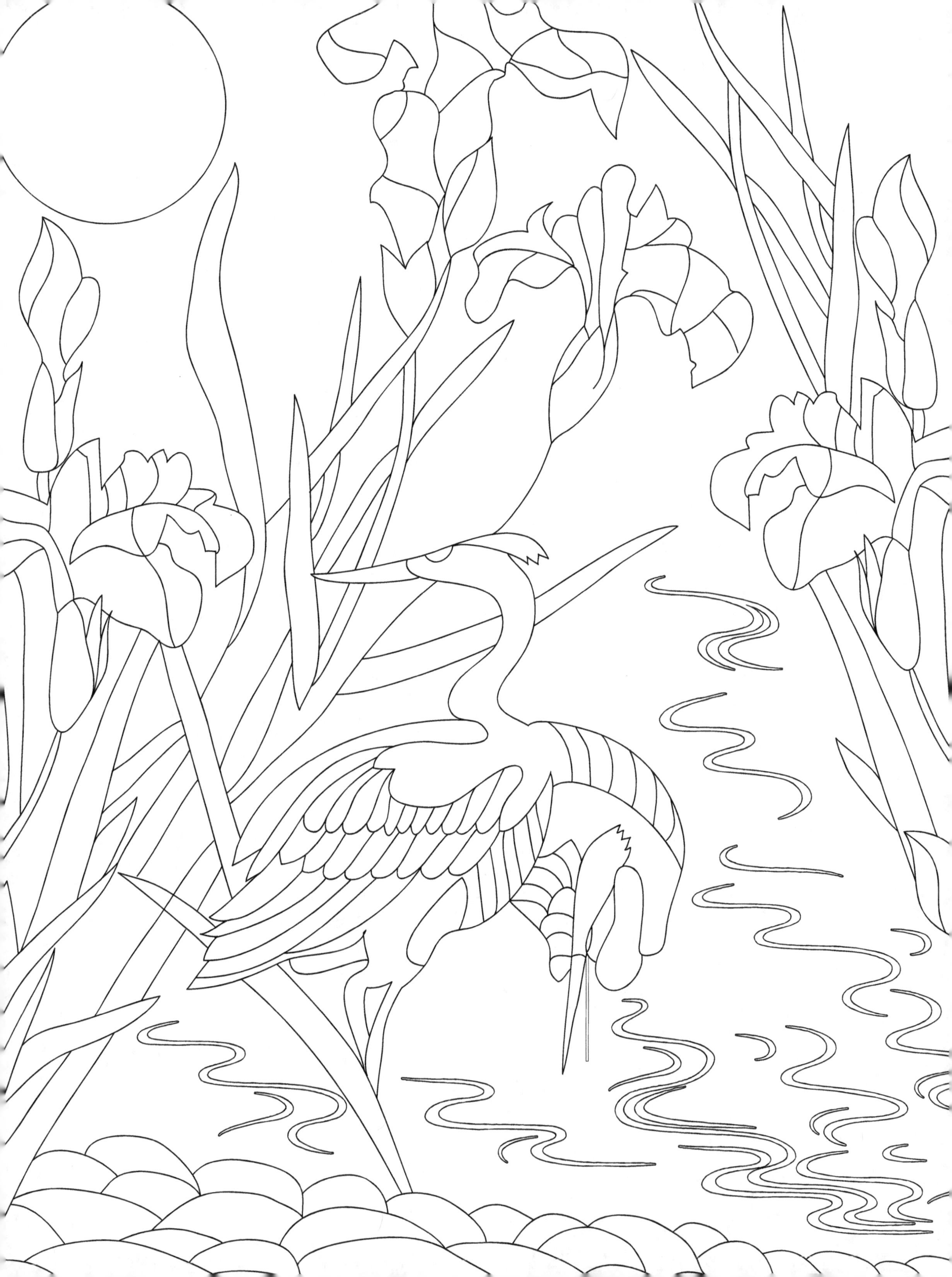

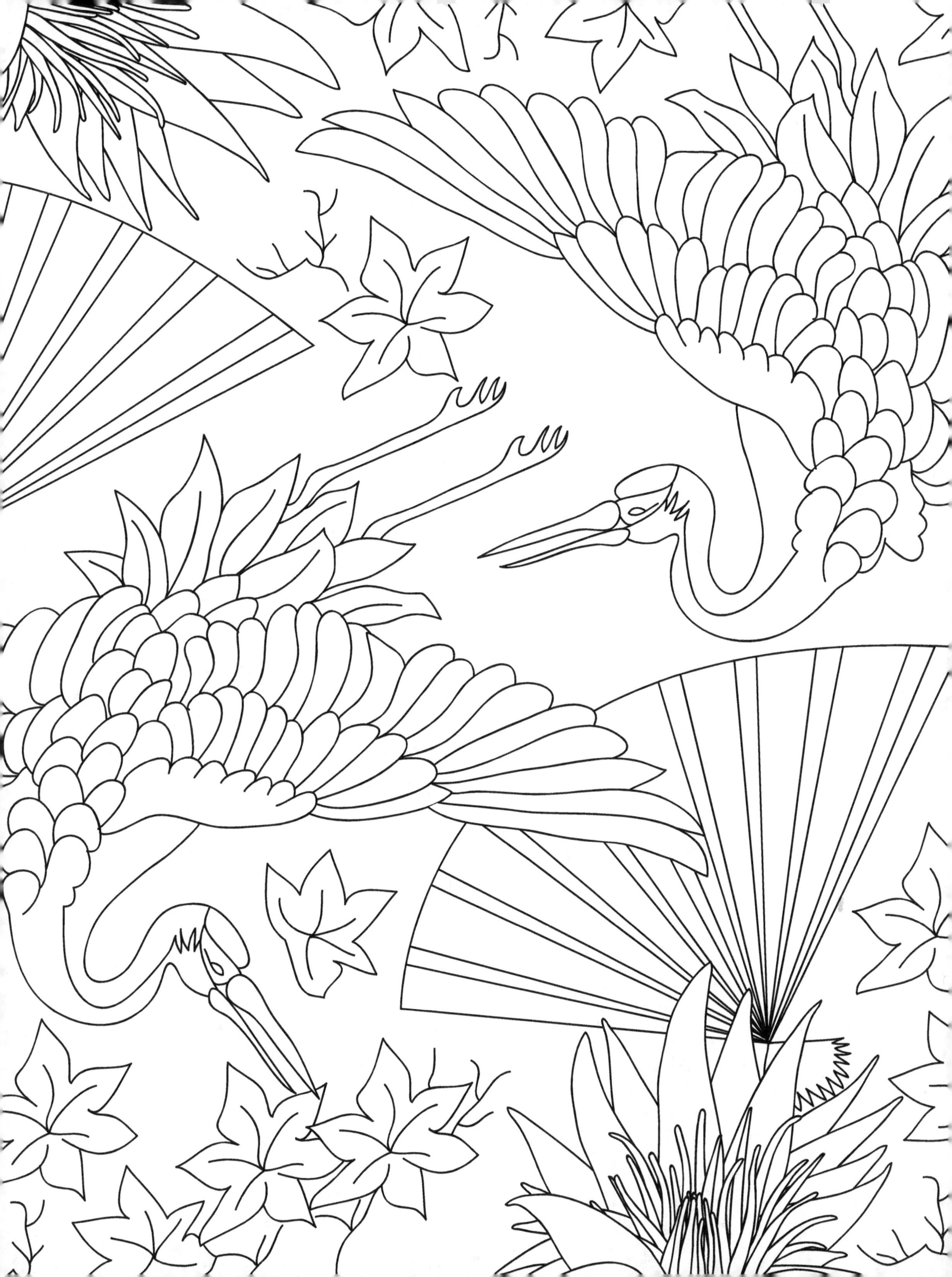

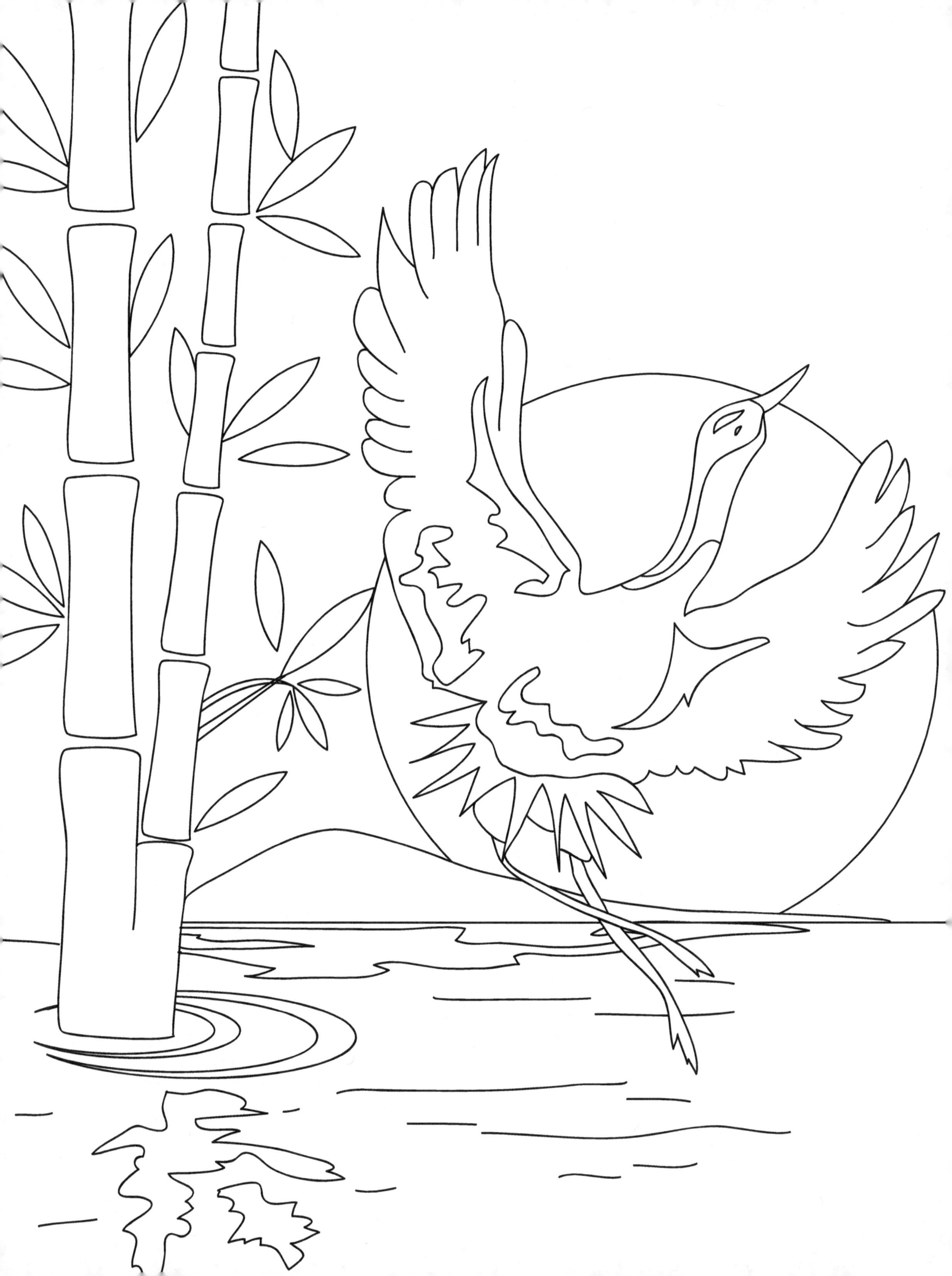

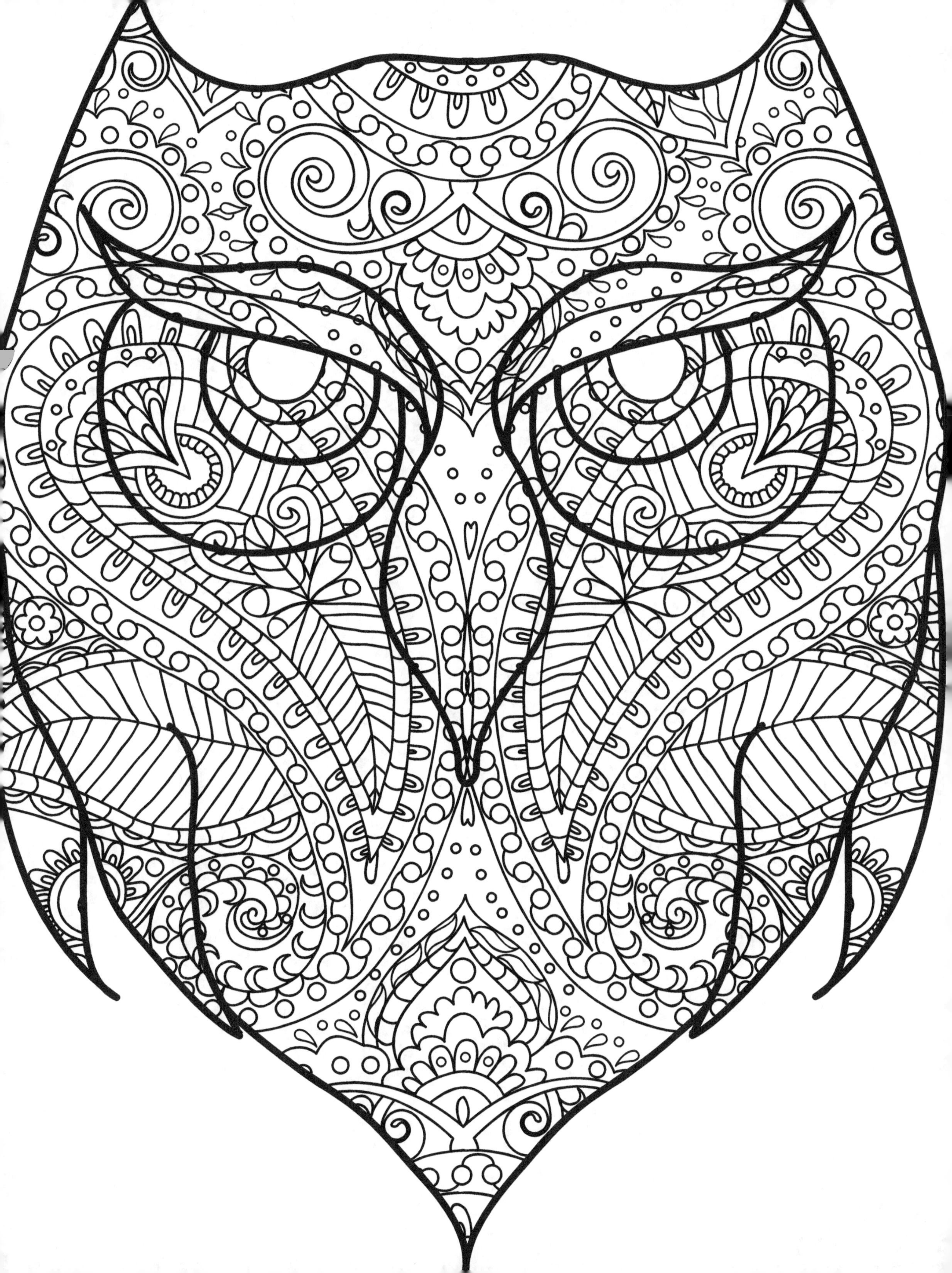

www.ingramcontent.com/pod-product-compliance
Lightning Source LLC
Chambersburg PA
CBHW081230280526
45787CB00006B/2596
* 9 7 8 1 5 1 7 7 8 8 4 7 6 *